THE FAMILY OF
JESUS CHRIST

by James Byers

The Family of Jesus Christ
by James Byers

The Family of Jesus Christ

Copyright @ 2016 by James Byers

ISBN-13: 978-0-9966962-8-9

Cover Design by Whitnee Clinard
Book Block Design by Whitnee Clinard

Published by Hilliard Press
a division of The Hilliard Institute
Franklin, Tennessee

Oxford, England
Abbeyleix, Ireland

www.hilliardinstitute.com.

THE FAMILY OF
JESUS CHRIST

by James Byers

HILLIARD
PRESS

TABLE OF CONTENTS

CHAPTER 5

CHAPTER 6

CHAPTER 7

CHAPTER 1

THE FEMALE GENEALOGY AND MARY

Matthew's Account

Telling the family history of Jesus is a complex task. Two of the gospel writers emphasize His life from the very beginning. Matthew approaches His genealogy with the history of Joseph, who is known as Jesus' legal father. Matthew's list of ancestors is divided into three sections. Matthew is dealing with a very important point: the legitimacy of Jesus' parentage. Jesus becomes known as the carpenter's son by the residents in Nazareth. It is charged—and the slander that is very early in origin—that Jesus is an illegitimate offspring of Mary.[1] To mesh the two beliefs that Jesus is miraculously conceived and that He is the heir of King David can "be done only on the basis of Joseph's genealogy, for whatever the lineage of Mary, Joseph was the head of the family, and the Davidic connection of Jesus could only be established by acknowledgement of Him as legal son by Joseph."[2]

Louis Sweet in his article about the genealogy observes the insertion of the names of certain women in Matthew's account. The

practice would be "abhorrent to ordinary usage."(3) The women
mentioned are a varied group. A.B. Bruce in his commentary
writes about the women, "concerning whom one might have
expected the genealogy to observe discreet silence: Tamar, Rahab,
Ruth, Bathsheba; three of them sinful women, and one Ruth, a
foreigner."(4)

Tamar is the first of the four questionable women in the ancestry
of Jesus. Her story is told in Genesis and reveals that she does not
have heirs after her marriage to the sons of Judah. Tamar hears
that Judah, her father-in-law, who is a widower as she is a widow,
is visiting in the area where she lives. She disguises herself as a
prostitute and conceives twin boys with Judah as the father. The
descendant in Matthew's list is Perez. Matthew includes Tamar
and Perez in the genealogy of Jesus to predict His care for the
hopeless. Tamar was a victim of being without children, and the
levirate marriage tradition had not been successful. Tamar had
to resort to her own ingenuity to ensure the continuity of her
family.

A different but nontraditional woman appears in Matthew's
ancestral family of Jesus. Rahab's story occurs over four hundred
years later as the Hebrew nation is planning its entrance into
Canaan. The fortress city of Jericho stands in the way. Joshua,
who is the consummate military leader and who had succeeded
Moses, knows taking Jericho will be no easy task. He sends two
spies who find lodging in the house of Rahab. Rahab is described
as a prostitute. The Greek translation in the Septuagint is *porne*.
This word's primary meaning is a prostitute with a secondary
meaning that she was also an innkeeper. Her house would have
been part of the fortress.

When the king of Jericho finds out about the spies, Rahab is
commanded to turn them over. Rahab then creates a fantastic
lie about the spies, telling the authorities that she does not know
where the spies came from and that they had left. Meanwhile she
is concealing the spies and afterwards reveals to them she knows
Yahweh has given the land to Israel. She confesses her fear for her

safety, for she has heard of the Red Sea crossing and the destruction of the Amorite tribe. She then makes a covenant with the spies so that she and her family will be spared if she doesn't reveal the mission of the spies and will stay in her house with her family when Jericho is conquered. A scarlet cord is a sign that Rahab will reveal to the Israelites. Thus Rahab makes one of the great affirmations of faith in the Bible: "The Lord your God is God in heaven above and on earth below" (Joshua 2). In Hebrews 11, her faith is recorded in the New Testament. Matthew again includes an unusual choice in his genealogy. Jesus goes to the sinners and publicans in His ministry. Rahab is a great example of a changed life. The book of Joshua records her salvation and her future life as an Israelite (Joshua 6).

After the death of Joshua, the period of the Judges begins. This period is a violent one during which the people of Israel are captured and delivered on numerous occasions. During this period one of the true jewels appears in the Old Testament canon.

The Book of Ruth is extraordinary in that it is one of the only two books in the Biblical canon titled with a woman's name. Unlike the Book of Esther, Ruth lives in a pastoral region near Bethlehem after leaving the country of Moab. Ruth is a young widow who is devoted to her mother-in-law, Naomi. Naomi decides to return to Bethlehem after her sons die in Moab. Ruth, in one of the most moving passages of the book, expresses her love for Naomi and her wish to go with her to Bethlehem. Famine had been in Israel and had forced Naomi, who was widowed, to the land of Moab. However, Ruth has known no other land but Moab. When Ruth goes with Naomi back to Israel, she goes as a foreigner.

Naomi knows about a man called Boaz, a wealthy landowner who is her relative. Naomi makes sure that Ruth works in the fields of Boaz at harvest time. Eventually Boaz and Ruth marry. The matter of levirate marriage enters into the picture as it did during the story of Tamar. Boaz legally becomes the redeemer of Ruth, whose deceased husband, Mahlon, was related to Boaz.

CHAPTER 1

Boaz states, "Today you are witnesses that I have bought from Naomi all the property of Elimelech, Kilion, and Mahlon. I have also acquired Ruth the Moabitess, Mahlon's widow, as my wife, in order to maintain the name of the dead with his property, so that his name will not disappear from among his family or from the town records" (Ruth 4).

All of this might appear as simply a happy ever after love story, but God's providence is seen in the genealogical table. Ruth is the great grandmother of David, the King. The story of Ruth fits well into the ancestral family of Jesus. Ruth is seen as a foreigner, not an Israelite, who is accepted into the nation. Ruth displays character and integrity beyond the other women mentioned. Yet, as an outsider, she reflects the desire of Jesus to include the foreigner into His family of believers. He heals the Gadarene possessed of demons (Matthew 8) and converses with the Samaritan woman (John 4). The story of Ruth leads us to the best known of the four women mentioned in Matthew's genealogy.

Matthew in his account writes, "David was the father of Solomon whose mother had been Uriah's wife" (1:6). The immediate question would be why did Matthew fail to mention Bathsheba's name and use the term "Uriah's wife" instead? In the case of the other women that have been mentioned, names are given. Would this be a condemnation of David or Bathsheba or both?

The story of David's adultery with Bathsheba is well known and is recorded in II Samuel 11:1-3:

> In the spring, at the time when kings go off to war,
> David sent Joab out with the king's men and the
> whole Israelite army. One evening David got up
> from his bed and walked around on the roof of the
> palace. From the roof he saw a woman bathing. The
> woman was very beautiful, and David sent someone
> to find out about her.

The story then moves quickly. David sends for her, and they have sexual relations. After Bathsheba informs David that she is pregnant, David begins to formulate elaborate schemes to cover up his sin. David removes Uriah from battle and sends him home to Bathsheba. Uriah, mindful of the sacrifices of his fighting peers who are still at war, refuses the comforts of home and sleeps with servants of the king instead of in the arms of his wife. Then David with cunning purpose gets Uriah drunk at a feast, but Uriah still refuses to go home. As a last resort, David sends Uriah back into battle and commands his general, Joab, to withdraw from protecting Uriah in battle to ensure his death. After a period of mourning, Bathsheba is brought to the palace of David where she becomes his wife. The scriptures say that "the thing David had done displeased the Lord" (11:27).

This story has both immediate and far-reaching consequences. Bathsheba and David's child dies. The prophet Nathan, who had predicted this tragedy, also tells David that violence will always be in his house. Bathsheba later gives birth to Solomon, and in the later days of David's life, she works to place their son Solomon in a position to become the next king.

In I Kings 1:17, with the advice of Nathan she implores David with these words: "My lord, you yourself swore to me your servant by the Lord your God: 'Solomon your son shall be king after me, and he will sit on my throne.'" It becomes obvious that Bathsheba risks the fate of herself and her son if Solomon is not made king. "Otherwise, as soon as my lord the king is laid to rest with his father, I and my son Solomon will be treated as criminals" (1:21). Her brilliant presentation persuades the king, and David says, "'As surely as the Lord lives, who has delivered me out of every trouble, I will surely carry out today what I swore to you by the Lord, The God of Israel: Solomon your son shall be king after me, and he will sit on my throne in my place.' Then Bathsheba bowed low with her face to the ground and kneeling before the king said, 'May my lord King David live forever'" (1:29-31). Of the four women mentioned, Bathsheba's role is the most complex. More sinned against than a sinner, she demonstrates

CHAPTER 1

the great forgiveness of God, and Matthew must have had this in mind when he included her in the ancestry of Jesus.

These four women are part of the ancestry of Jesus and His family. These four women are included, and they have unusual stories—stories reflective of Christ's message and manner. Matthew, although Jewish, reveals the inclusive nature of Jesus' mission by including women: some who were not of Jewish background, and all who had less than perfect backgrounds.

Luke's Account

When Luke examines the ancestry of Jesus, he chooses Mary's family. Luke's ancestry differs from Matthew's account in several ways. Luke does not immediately begin with the genealogy but waits until Jesus' ministry to include a family tree. A.B. Bruce comments in *The Expositor's Greek Testament* that the "Davidic sonship, it is true remains, but it cannot be vital to the Messiahship of One who is in the sense of the Gospel, Son of God. It becomes like the moon when the sun is shining."[5]

As mentioned, the emphasis of Luke leans toward the family of Mary whose father is named Eli. Both genealogies cross at the name Shealtiel and his son Zerubbabel and later with the mention of David as the father of Solomon in Matthew's listing. However, Luke records David as the father of Nathan, another of David's sons, in his genealogy.

Some have questioned if the genealogy listed in Luke belongs to Mary or Joseph. To examine the conjecture that Luke chose to follow Mary's heritage, Louis Sweet states, "The authorities have been divided as to whether Lk's genealogy is Joseph's as appears, or Mary's."[6] To follow this logic would explain the apparent choice of Joseph's ancestry and also the visit of Mary with Joseph to Bethlehem at the time of the registration.[7] Sweet concludes, "It is further to be noticed that in the annunciation (Luke 1:32) the promised One is called at once Son of God and Son of David, and that He is the Son of God by virtue of His conception by the Spirit—leaving it evident that He is the Son of David, and that He is the Son of God by virtue of His birth of Mary."[8]

The result is Jesus is a descendant as the Son of God and a descendant of the legal and physical lineage of David. The opinion of Mary as a descendant of David also fits with Luke's inclusion of the Gentile world, and the appeal of Jesus' coming into the world for both Jew and non-Jew.

Of all the family members, Mary has the greatest influence in modern times. Generations of believers have been fascinated with her and her selection as the mother of Jesus. The name "Mary" is a common one in both testaments. For example, Mary of Bethany and Mary of Magdala are well known in the New Testament. The Hebrew name for Mary is Miriam, and the Miriam of prominence in the Old Testament is the sister of Moses.

Mary is pictured in Luke's Gospel as a maiden of Nazareth. Tradition names her mother as Anna. The Crusaders built a lovely church in Anna's homage in Jerusalem. The church is still standing and open to visitors. Other ancestors of Mary are really unknown unless one interprets Luke's genealogy as that of Mary. Her town of Nazareth was unimportant in her day and is even described with these words, "Can anything good come from Nazareth?" (John 1:46). These references make the selection of Mary baffling. Furthermore, she would have little education, and would not have been prominent in social standing. Despite these considerations, Luke records that an angel named Gabriel appears to her. This maiden, still quite young, is selected by God to be the mother of Jesus, the Messiah, and The Son of God.

Naturally the visit of Gabriel disturbs her. Mary is already betrothed, a strong word in those days. She is troubled, but with calm piety as she believes the words of the angel. Mary quite logically explains her plight to Gabriel. The angel continues to encourage her. How Mary understands these words is still open

CHAPTER 1

to speculation. Did she first interpret that this child would be a great king who would rule Israel? The greatest question lingered, "How can this happen? I am not married?" (Luke 1:24). Gabriel states, in what is now an often-quoted verse, "Nothing is impossible for God" (Luke 1:37). The angel is sympathetic. Gabriel knows that Mary needs encouragement from another woman. He mentions Mary's relative Elizabeth who is pregnant and who is also experiencing a miraculous event. Mary makes the statement that shows a great faith: "Let it be according to your word" (Luke 1:38).[9] Her quiet submission to the will of God is unsurpassed, even when experiencing the problems of future conversations with Joseph, her husband to be. As the commentator Leon Morris concludes, "She recognized the will of God and accepted it."[10]

Mary is just beginning the great changes that occur in her life. Gabriel's aforestated mention of Elizabeth to Mary encourages the latter to visit her relative. The Greek word for their relationship can be translated as "kinswoman," which could mean a close or even distant cousin. In all likelihood, Elizabeth is old enough to be an aunt.

Mary goes quickly to see Elizabeth, probably accompanied by others, and receives great praise. Elizabeth recognizes the superior blessing that has been bestowed on Mary. In fact, she says Mary is blessed above all women. Morris comments that there is an absence of jealousy on the part of Elizabeth. She is the older woman, but in genuine humility recognizes the greater blessing God has given Mary. Morris writes, "a further point of interest is that John the Baptist did not recognize Jesus as the Messiah until the baptism. Apparently Elizabeth's recognition that he is Lord was inspired, but personal. John had to find it out for himself."[11]

After absorbing the blessing of Elizabeth, Mary sings praise to God. Luke may have known Mary in her later years and heard this song. The song has been called the "Magnificat" or song of praise. In the song Mary expresses her gratitude to God for blessing her. Mary describes herself in the song as a humble servant (Luke 1:48). The word in Greek literally means a slave.

She extends God's blessing toward everyone who worships Him. She sings, "God drags strong rulers from their thrones and puts humble people in places of power. God gives the hungry good things to eat, and sends the rich away with nothing. God helps His servant Israel and is always merciful to His people. The Lord made this promise to our ancestors, to Abraham and his family forever!" (Luke 1:51-55). The last lines of the song reverse the prevailing ideas of the social status of humanity. The humble will be exalted while the Lord scatters the proud and overturns rulers. God will feed those in need and send the wealthy away with nothing. Mary believes that this revelation will exalt her nation Israel. It is highly unlikely that she thought beyond her own people.

Mary's hardest trip had to be her return to Nazareth after her visit with Elizabeth. She likely lived in Elizabeth's home until the birth of John the Baptist. When Mary returns home, she has to meet with Joseph, her betrothed. She must have been very anxious for his reaction to her story. Mary knows the punishment for adultery is severe, even resulting at times in death. All things being possible with God must have been in her mind. The Gospel of Matthew reveals Joseph's kindness, as he plans to divorce her quietly, and his own angel visit, which shares the truth of Mary's situation (Matthew 1:18-23). Through Joseph's actions, Mary must have recognized that she was marrying a kind and generous man, one of great faith who would be with her in all of her struggles.

After her full acceptance by Joseph, another difficult journey has to be made to Bethlehem to register for a census. David, the King, was an ancestor of Joseph, and Joseph had to be registered in his ancestral home. This unexpected trip for Mary, whom some conjecture went with Joseph so he could protect her from those who had suspicions about the legitimacy of her child, is long, especially for a pregnant woman. The Gospel of Luke continues to tell the birth story in simple language. The couple finds no place to lodge in Bethlehem. They finally find a stable or cave. As Morris writes, the birth of Jesus "points to poverty, obscurity, and

CHAPTER 1

rejection. That Mary wrapped the child herself points to a lonely birth."[12]

Mary's role as mother to Jesus is difficult. She and her husband, Joseph, flee to Egypt to escape the fury of Herod, the ruling king. Both parents protect Jesus for an unknown period of time before returning to Nazareth. The scriptures describe Mary as a thoughtful mother. Luke records the journey of the family to Jerusalem for the Passover feast. When Jesus, who is twelve at the time, disappears from their company, Mary is very concerned, even angry that He is missing. When found, Jesus explains that He is attending to His Father's concerns while at the temple. This occasion prepares Mary for future events. Luke ends his comments on the youth of Jesus by saying that Jesus matures in every way: intellectually, physically, spiritually, and socially (Luke 2:52).

Mary During the Ministry Years

After the so-called "lost years," Jesus appears in His ministry at an age of approximately thirty. By this time Mary has begun to understand the special powers that her son possesses. In John's Gospel, Mary and Jesus appear at a wedding feast in the village of Cana. B.F. Westcott, a distinguished scholar of the New Testament, believes that Mary is closely connected with the wedding party and is at the wedding festivities well before Jesus arrives.[13] Westcott thinks that Mary, in her later years and under the care of John the Apostle, reveals the details of this story to him. John reminds his readers that this event at Cana includes the first miracle of Jesus, and Westcott mentions that this miracle places Mary in a prominent place.[14]

During the ministry of Jesus, Mary appears at different times. The book of Mark records an incident when she and the brothers of Jesus attempt to restrain His activity and direct Him to a period of "retirement for a time," encouraged by "loving anxiety," as Louis Sweet describes the concern.[15] Mary is seemingly still unclear as to the mission of Jesus. Mary no doubt can remember the prophecy of Simeon that her soul would be pierced (Luke 2:35). She has heard from Jesus that His true relatives are in the kingdom of heaven (Matthew 12:48-50). Mary has to experience the entire ministry of her Son to know that He is indeed the promised Messiah, and to understand what that entails. When the occasion is the darkest, Mary is there at the crucifixion of her Son. She and the others at the cross can do little. They cannot speak before the Sanhedrin for the defense of Jesus. They cannot appeal to the Roman Procurator, Pontius Pilate. They cannot stop the angry mob or overpower the Roman guards. Yet, Mary stays at the cross as He dies (Matthew 27:55-56; Mark 15:40-41; John 19:25-27).

His burial rites must have included Mary. The tomb for Jesus had been given to Mary's family by Joseph of Arimathea, a member of the Sanhedrin. Luke mentions a plurality of women at the tomb (23:55). From every indication, Mary is an early witness of the resurrection. She must have been among the over 500 to whom Jesus appeared.

Mary is also mentioned at the beginning of the Book of Acts. From all indications Mary becomes one of the members of the Jerusalem fellowship and lives the rest of her life with John the Apostle as her chief caretaker. F.F. Bruce, the prominent and prolific religious commentator, writes concerning Acts 1:14, "This is the last recorded appearance of the Mother of our Lord. It is significant that she is found in prayer with His disciples."[16]

Mary comes full circle. The angel's message prophesies her favor with God and the birth of her Son. She lives to see or hear of the angels' appearance to the women at the tomb. She witnesses the resurrected Jesus, and she worships with the believers in Jerusalem.

CHAPTER 1

CHAPTER 2

JOSEPH, THE LEGAL FATHER

Joseph, who is described in the Gospels of Matthew and Luke as the earthly father of Jesus, can be called the invisible man of his family. The New Testament has no quotation from him. However, the gospel accounts of Joseph do regard him as an essential parent in the rearing of Jesus. Angels actually appear to him more than Mary. He, above all others, is entrusted with the protection of Jesus as well as His earthly instruction.

Matthew introduces Joseph to us as a man perplexed by the pregnancy of his fiancée Mary. He contemplates a quiet divorce rather than a more severe punishment. While this anxiety is weighing upon him, an angel reveals that Mary's baby was conceived of the Holy Spirit. The angel instructs Joseph to marry his betrothed. Further instructions include naming the baby "Jesus" because He will save His people from their sins (Matthew 1:20, 21). Luke's account emphasizes the betrothal. Morris offers the opinion, "Perhaps because, though they were married, the marriage was not yet consummated."[17]

The marriage ceremony takes place, but the scriptures do not reveal where or who is in attendance. Customs of the time dictate there would have been a marriage supper, generally in the home of the groom. This marriage would have affected family and friends in different ways. The people of Nazareth know the family and acknowledge in later times that Jesus is the carpenter's son. Is there a certain amount of stigma attached to the proceeding? How much support from the community does the couple receive? These are questions that are not answered in the scriptures, but one must conclude that Joseph and Mary must have had strong faith in God, no matter the reactions of those around them.

After the birth of Jesus, Matthew 1:25 refers to the consummation of the marriage. R.T. France in his commentary writes, "The marriage was thus formally completed, but not consummated before the birth of Jesus. There is no biblical warrant for the tradition of the perpetual virginity of Mary."[18]

In Luke's account of the birth, there is the story as previously mentioned of the difficult journey to Bethlehem to take part in a Roman Census. Luke's account is concise in nature, "Mary was engaged to Joseph and traveled with him to Bethlehem. She was going to have a baby, and while they were there, she gave birth to her first-born son" (Luke 1:5-7).

Luke also mentions that, after arrival, they find no place to lodge in Bethlehem. The birth takes place in a stable or attached dwelling place, the lowliness of which cannot be disregarded. As previously mentioned, Morris emphasizes the total obscurity and poverty of the birth scene.[19]

Joseph continues being the superb husband and earthly father during this time. And then more assurance comes. God sends His angels not to kings or rulers, but to shepherds. Shepherds were working class and sometimes not of the best reputation. Yet the angels deliver to them words of great joy. "'Don't be afraid! I have good news for you, which will make everyone happy. This very day in King David's hometown a Savior was born to you. He is Christ the Lord. You will know who He is, because you will find Him dressed in baby clothes and lying on a bed of hay.' Suddenly

CHAPTER 2

many other angels came down from heaven and joined in praising God. They said, 'Praise God in heavens! Peace on earth to everyone who pleases God'" (Luke 2:10-14).

Joseph remains a protector of Jesus during the infancy years. This invisible man doubtless oversees the rite of circumcision. Years pass, and Jesus is visited by the Magi, or wise men, from the East. By this time Joseph has made Bethlehem his home as J.W. McGarvey writes, "Joseph intended to make Bethlehem his home in the future."[20] The Magi leave their precious gifts. It may be assumed that Joseph uses the gifts wisely, especially the gold. During the glorious visit of the Magi, King Herod becomes suspicious of their visit. At this time in his rule, Herod fears a rebellion. Herod even kills family members out of paranoid fear.

Herod takes the Magi seriously. He realizes that many Jews are looking for a Messiah to be a great military and political leader. Herod calls together his priests and scribes in hope these experts in Jewish law can tell him where a possible usurper to his throne would be born. In Matthew 2:6, the priests provide him with a verse from Micah, a prophet from the Old Testament. "But you Bethlehem, in the land of Judah, are by no means least among the rulers of Judah; for out of you will come a ruler who will be the shepherd of my people Israel" (Micah 5:2).

Now Herod plans to use the Magi from the East along with the expertise of his Jewish scholars to eradicate the danger. But the Lord warns the Magi, and they return to their homes by a different route, ignoring Herod's false request: "Go and search carefully for the child. As soon as you find him, report to me, so that I too may go and worship him" (Matthew 2:8). In a short time an angel appears to Joseph, and he leaves Judea for Egypt. Joseph, just as he had reacted when he heard the message to wed Mary, obeys the message and acts immediately (2:14).

The length of time that Joseph and Mary spend in Egypt is not mentioned, only that they stay until Herod dies (2:15). However, this period of time must have been a time of reflection for the family. Although Joseph has left no verbal record of his thoughts, his actions are always obedient to the words of his God.

Joseph is mentioned in the scriptures only a few times after the flight to Egypt. He leads the family to the Passover Feast in Luke 2. Jesus is no longer an infant but a young man. During this feast visit in Jerusalem, Jesus becomes lost to the family. Finally, they find Him in the Temple discussing the Mosaic Law with religious leaders. Leon Morris opines that at this point in time, "Jesus had a relationship to God shared by no other. Mary and Joseph did not understand this."[21] Joseph must have remembered the angel's protective warnings, and now he is witnessing the maturity of Jesus as He is found in the Temple.

Since Joseph is not included with Mary and her family in the scriptures following this Passover trip, he seems to disappear from the family. As was the patriarch custom of that day, he most likely teaches Jesus the trade of carpentry. Luke mentions that Jesus grows in wisdom and stature and favor with God and man (2:52). Joseph is a sensitive man, perhaps not as reflective as Mary. He is fervent in keeping the Mosaic Law. He would assure that Jesus has training in the synagogue schools. Thus Joseph fulfills a unique position as the earthly father of Jesus in the most admirable way possible. Conjecture about his life beyond his appearance with Jesus at the Passover feast cannot be verified. But it can always be said that he followed the instructions of Yahweh in the care and protection of Jesus.

CHAPTER 2

CHAPTER 3

THE BROTHERS OF JESUS

Mentions of the Siblings of Jesus

As noted previously, Matthew very plainly states that Joseph and Mary had marital relations after the birth of Jesus (Matthew 1:25). Most scholars today believe that Joseph and Mary had children. If so, these children would be younger than Jesus. In Matthew 13:55, 56, the writer records Jesus visiting his hometown of Nazareth. "Isn't he the son of the carpenter? Isn't Mary his mother, and aren't James, Joseph, Simon, and Judas his brothers? Don't his sisters still live in our town?" Since Joseph is absent from the latter part of the Gospels, the speculation goes that Joseph dies before the ministry of Jesus. The family of Jesus now has the responsibility for the care of their mother. Circumstances change when Jesus assumes His ministry. After the wedding feast at which Jesus performs His first miracle, He goes with His mother, brothers, and disciples to the town of Capernaum "where they stayed for a few days" (John 2:11-12). Alfred Plummer identifies these brothers as the children of Joseph and Mary: "There is nothing in scripture to forbid the natural view that the brothers are the children of

Joseph and Mary, born after the birth of Jesus." Plummer further states that, at this time, there is little evidence that Jesus' siblings, including James, are believers in the Messiahship of Christ. His mother expresses faith in His power to perform miracles. She also ponders or thinks deeply about other events. How much she believes in His Messiahship at this point is unclear. However, the brothers of Jesus are not yet true disciples.[22]

Even so, Mary and the brothers continue to attempt to protect Jesus:

> Jesus decided to leave Judea and to start going through Galilee because the leaders of the people wanted to kill him. It was time for the Festival of the Shelters, and Jesus' brothers said to Him, "Why don't you go to Judea? Then your disciples can see what you are doing. No one does anything in secret, if they want others to know about them. So let the world know what you are doing!" Even Jesus' own brothers had not become His followers. Jesus answered, "My time hasn't yet come, but your time is always here. The people of the world cannot hate you. They hate me, because I tell them that they do evil things. Go on to the festival. My time hasn't yet come, and I am not going." Jesus said this and stayed on in Galilee. (John 7:1-9)

Another passage in Mark 3:20, 21 indicates that His family wants to control His behavior. In Matthew 12:46-50 His family wants to see Him, and He says, "These are my mother and my brothers. Anyone who obeys my Father in heaven is my brother or sister or mother." Though His family didn't always understand Him, all of these passages demonstrate their concern for Him. There is the passage in John 7:5 that explains even His brothers did not believe in Him (*ouk episteuon*), which has always been troubling. The commentator John Painter has defined the loyalty to Jesus by His siblings as less than ideal.[23]

CHAPTER 3

This lack of complete faith is present even until the time of the crucifixion. The conclusion at this point in time is simply that James, Jesus' other siblings, and most of the disciples were frightened, dismayed, and uncertain. Painter acknowledges that, from the beginning, His family members were always followers of Jesus in various ways. Yet the fire of zeal takes time to be refined. The events following the crucifixion have a profound effect on James and other disciples. They undergo a profound and complete change.

The resurrection of Jesus Christ is recorded in all of the Gospels. In I Corinthians 15:5-8, Paul the Apostle mentions the many resurrection appearances of Jesus including Peter and James, the brother of Jesus, as well as his own vision. In the particular experience of James, details of the appearance are not revealed. One can only conclude that what was lacking in the belief of James is changed forever by this experience. James no longer considers Jesus just as his earthly brother. He also considers Him his Lord and Savior. Paul writes that more than five hundred people see Jesus after His resurrection. The transformation of the resurrected Christ dramatically changes the lives of these witnesses.

James, the Brother of Jesus

In Acts, Luke mentions James: "The apostles often met together and prayed with a single purpose in mind. The women and Mary the mother of Jesus would meet with them, and so would his brothers" (Acts: 1:14). In these early days and weeks of the church assembly, it appears that apostles led the small assembly in worship.

The next time James is mentioned is in Acts 12 where the release of Peter from prison is recounted. Herod Agrippa, the grandson of Herod the Great, has executed James, the son of Zebedee, and Peter appears to be next in line. But an angel releases Peter from prison and directs him to the streets of Jerusalem. Peter goes to a house church meeting at the home (*oikion*) of John Mark's mother. The church gathers at this home and is praying for Peter's release, and all are startled to find him knocking at their door. As F.F. Bruce comments, the church members are surprised "to believe that their own prayers have been answered so quickly" as they listen to "Rhoda's (a servant girl) insistence that it really was Peter—while all the time the poor man himself stands anxiously knocking for admission."[24]

The year of Peter's imprisonment is in the early 40s A.D. After his release, Peter makes a significant statement to his disciples. He tells them to keep quiet, but he also says, "Tell James and the others what happened" (Acts 12:17). By this time James has become a leader in the church of Jerusalem. This James is obviously the brother of Jesus because James, the son of Zebedee and brother of John, had recently been executed.

In his essay entitled "James and Jesus on Israel and Purity," Scott McKnight concludes, "A more careful examination of the data shows that James was indeed a significant, a (perhaps the) dominant leader of the Jerusalem Church and the spokesman for the earliest form of Jerusalem based Christian Judaism. For instance, from Acts 1:4 and Acts 12:17 we can infer that the brothers of Jesus were both at the chronological basis of the Jerusalem churches as well as the core leaders of the movement."[25]

In Acts 15, Luke records a conference or meeting—a forerunner of later Christian councils. Changes are occurring in the early fellowship. A successful mission trip had been undertaken in the great city of Antioch, Syria. The success of the Antioch mission, which means that there might soon be more Gentile Christians in the world than Jewish Christians, creates a serious problem. F.F. Bruce considers James's role at the conference a pivotal one. Bruce notices that Peter and the other apostles are increasingly absent from Jerusalem. Ten years have transpired since Peter's release from prison, and the year is close to 50 A.D. Bruce acknowledges the success of the conference and writes, "It was in considerable part thanks to James' practical wisdom that a

CHAPTER 3

serious problem, which might have brought about an unbridge-able cleavage in primitive Christianity, was settled in a spirit of concord." This conference is never surpassed in importance in its implications for the future of Christianity. F.F. Bruce recognizes that problems had festered for years. He cites Peter's refusal to participate in a fellowship meal with Gentiles, and Paul's subsequent criticism of Peter's hypocrisy. Bruce also mentions the early experience of the church in regards to mandatory observance of Jewish ceremonial law including male circumcision. Paul had written an acerbic letter to Galatian converts who were submitting to Jewish customs.[26]

Thus the conference determines if Christianity can exist in an amicable manner with Jew and Gentile. The stakes are high because many of the new church congregations contained both Jewish and Gentile ethnic groups. After persuasive testimony from Peter regarding his own experiences—particularly his visit to Cornelius, a Roman Centurion, and the subsequent conversion of Cornelius and his household—the other members of the Jerusalem church accept the inclusion of Gentiles (Acts 15:6-11).

The conference, under the supervision of James, adopts a compromise that allows for customs to be observed without the main teachings of Christianity being thwarted. Most of the compromises were already observed at this time by all Christians, whether Jew or Gentile: including refraining from idolatry; adhering to strict morality including righteous behavior regarding sexual relationships; and not eating blood meat (Acts 15:28-29). The art of selective compromise works beautifully, and James's admonition must have been received with great appreciation.

James asserts his moral authority in a global way. His conduct at the conference shows a man willing to listen before giving advice. The conference also documents that James, above all other leaders, has credibility as Jesus' brother to speak with authority. Even such stalwarts as Peter and Paul are satisfied with James's instructions. The church, even though more Jewish in some areas and more Gentile in others, becomes one church.

After the historic conference in which James acts as counselor and decision maker, little is mentioned of him in the scriptures. In all likelihood James increases in importance not only in Jerusalem, but throughout the community of believers. With the inclusion of the Epistle of James into the New Testament canon, more evidence of his religious beliefs is revealed.

The Epistle of James

The Letter of James does not identify the author. The main contenders for authorship are James, the brother of Jesus, or James, the son of Zebedee. James Zebedee is martyred early on in the history of the New Testament. His death occurs about 44 A.D. at the hands of Herod Agrippa. This leaves James, the brother of Jesus, as the likely author.

J.W. Roberts in his commentary about the epistle strongly favors the brother of Jesus. Roberts emphasizes the close connection of family ties. "It may be safely concluded that James is an actual brother to Jesus in the flesh through the common mother, Mary."[27] Roberts concedes that, during the ministry of Jesus, James and other family members have their doubts as to the Messiahship of Jesus but concludes the following:

> After the resurrection Christ appeared to James (I Cor. 15:7) and this seems to have changed all, for immediately it is noted that he was among the number who waited during the interval before Pentecost (Acts 1:13,14). James' attitude could be described as typical of Judaistic Christianity. First his Hebrew or Jewish background is taken as basic. But he is also seen in the dual role of championing the freedom of the Gentiles from the law (as Paul contended) while at the same time being zealous for the observance of traditional Judaism for Jewish Christians. This is probably to be interpreted as a measure of

statesmanship aimed at winning his nation to the claims of the gospel.[28]

The Epistle of James continues to have doubters as to authorship. One objection is that the Greek is too good for a native of Israel. This doubt is based on the specious assumption that Jesus' family could not have known Greek because the family lacked educational opportunities. Obviously, Greek-speaking Jews are in the Jerusalem church as Luke describes in Acts 6. A conclusion would have to be made that not only James but Peter and John who also wrote letters in the New Testament did not know Greek. Without a doubt, translators were available when needed. Another objection is that James makes few references to Jesus, only two in number, and never states the Lord is his brother. Yet these objections pale in significance when recognition is made of James's complete humility in regards to Jesus as Christ. Of course, by the time of the authorship of the letter, about 60 A.D., everyone in the Christian community would recognize James as not only the brother of Jesus but the foremost leader of the Jerusalem church.

The letter or epistle itself is a model of practical Christianity. If one is a Christian, how must one conduct one's life? This question is thoroughly answered by James in various ways and in various situations. James has as his main concern a definition of the Christian life. His readers are a scattered group. They are of Jewish ethnicities and encounter everything from persecution to affluence. He devotes a large portion of his letter to admonishing his readers to a life of endurance to hardship. He encourages them to hold on to their faith and ask for wisdom.

The letter of James is not a letter that is neatly organized. Various topics relating to Christian conduct are discussed. Roberts thinks that all the various themes of the letter relate to James 1:19-27, much as a piece of music has various expositions of a central theme.[29] In this passage James centers Christian conduct on controlling anger and subduing evil, placing stress on obedience to the word of God. James encourages what he calls **true religion**.

James talks about the controlling of one's speech in the third chapter of his epistle. Arrogance and personal cruelty are strongly condemned in chapter four. The epistle in chapter five is full of warnings for the rich and exhortations to the humble. James 5:4 summarizes his thoughts: "You refused to pay the people who worked in your fields, and now their unpaid wages are shouting out against you. The Lord All-Powerful has surely heard the cries of the workers who harvested your crops." In James 5:6 he writes, "You have condemned and murdered innocent people who couldn't even fight back."

James teaches patience, kindness, and prayerful supplications. He admonishes his listeners, "If you are having trouble, you should pray. And if you are feeling good, you should sing praises. If you are sick, ask the church leaders to come and pray for you" (James 5:13-14), and "if you turn sinners from the wrong way, you will save them from death, and many of their sins will be forgiven" (James 5:20).

In his summary of the thoughts in James's letter, Painter mentions that the teachings in James about God are "drawn from the riches of the Jewish tradition, rooted in an understanding of creation which finds itself confronted by evil and suffering. The Epistle of James has as its central concern a deep sympathy for the poor and persecuted. It advocates the rights of widows and orphans while offering a stern critique of the rich merchants and rich farmers."[30]

James shares the Jewish idea of the righteous person who will suffer and who will face temptation. The believer will face adversity just as the prophets, Job and Elijah to be specific, had. When looking at this type of language, we see James says many of the things that his brother Jesus had taught. Many subjects in James's letter were discussed by Jesus in His lifetime including The Law of Love, humility and exaltation, and relationship with brethren. James's epistle is not in disagreement with Paul's gospel message, as J.R.W. Stott makes clear. Stott writes, "Paul and James can be reconciled in their New Testament letters too. They taught the same way of salvation."[31] The apparent theological differences between Paul and James can be resolved when looking at the working faith extolled by Jesus. While primarily addressed to Jewish converts, James's epistle has now been more thoroughly understood as a truly "catholic" letter, a letter whose teachings affect all ethnic and social groups.

The End of James's Life

The final years of James's life end in his martyrdom, according to tradition, in Jerusalem about 62 or 63 A.D. Martyrdom had affected the early Christians in many ways. R. B. Rackham in his commentary on the book of Acts writes that "the death of Stephen was the crucial event which started the expansion of the church. The blood of the martyr was the seed of the church." As the Christians scatter during the first persecution, "they evangelized or preached the word. Thus as the chief strength of Judaism, both political and intellectual, lay in its Dispersion or Scattering abroad, so the new Dispersion of the Christians formed the progressive and missionary element in the church." The preacher Stephen sees "Jesus standing as Prophet and Mediator between God and man."[32]

The martyrdom of Stephen is the most dramatic of these early sacrificial deaths because it is the first recorded in the gospel narratives, and certainly because of Stephen's eloquent address. Other early martyrdoms follow. The missionary activity of Peter and James and John continues to be an influence in the Jerusalem area until this effort is violently interrupted by the execution of James, the son of Zebedee, described briefly by Luke in the Book of Acts. F.F. Bruce, in his book *The Spreading Flame*, comments:

> It is remarkable, indeed how little we know about
> the later career of most of the twelve apostles.
> James, the son of Zebedee, we know, was executed in
> Jerusalem under Herod Agrippa I in 44, we can trace

the movements of his brother John from time to
time, and we can reconstruct the outline of Peter's
later life with considerable probability. But what
do we know of Andrew and Thomas and Matthew,
Philip and Bartholomew, James the son of Alphaeus
and Judas the son of James, Simon the Zealot, and
Matthias, the successor of Judas Iscariot? Legend
is lavish in its willingness to tell us what became
of them, but we have amazingly little historical
knowledge. They do not appear to have remained in
Jerusalem after the middle of the first century.[33]

Bruce concludes that this martyrdom fires the repressive actions
taken against the "Nazarenes" and invigorates the zealous career
of Paul against this new doctrine and its adherents. This persecuted group, who is later called Christians, leaves Jerusalem "for
other parts of Judea and some even crossed the boundaries of
Palestine into Syria and Phoenicia and other neighboring states
and provinces."[34]

In the execution of James Zebedee, the Jewish ruler plays an important part. Herod Agrippa is the grandson of Herod the Great
and has close ties to Rome. He is friends with both Tiberius and
Caligula, the emperors. Tiberius rewards Agrippa. Rackham
comments that Herod Agrippa is "instrumental in getting the
senate to accept Claudius as his successor, and the grateful emperor added to Agrippa's kingdom Judea and Samaria. Agrippa
had hitherto remained at Rome, where he had been notorious
chiefly for his prodigality and extravagance. Now he returned to
his kingdom of Judea, and there, in order to gain the favour of
the Jews, he displayed the greatest assiduity in the observance of
the law and the exhibition of external righteousness."[35] Another
martyrdom is mentioned before the Christian era of Stephen
and James Zebedee. The Gospel of Matthew records the most
complete account of the execution of John called the Baptist. (For
more detail on this topic, see "The Death of John the Baptist" in
chapter five.)

CHAPTER 3

The execution of James, the brother of Jesus, is not mentioned in scripture. According to Eusebius, a church historian who wrote the *Ecclesiastical History* some two hundred years after the death of Jesus, James's execution is carried out by certain radical Jewish leaders. Certain Pharisees call upon James to denounce Jesus as the Christ, and James will not comply. James comments, "Why do ye ask me respecting Jesus the Son of Man? He is now sitting in the heavens, on the right hand of great Power, and is about to come on the clouds of heaven." In Eusebius's account, this seals the fate of James, who is tossed from the Temple by the radical Scribes and Pharisees who hear this. Eusebius adds that James is also clubbed with a heavy object to ensure his death. "So admirable a man indeed as James, and so celebrated among all for his justice, that even the wiser part of the Jews were of the opinion that this was the cause of the immediate siege of Jerusalem, which happened to them for no other reason than the crime against him."[36]

Judas / Jude

James had a brother called Judas or Jude. Paul refers to Jude as the brother of the Lord (I Corinthians 9:5). Matthew records the comments of the people of Nazareth: "Isn't Mary his mother and aren't James, Joseph, Simon, and Judas his brothers?" (Matthew 13:55-56). Other knowledge of Jude comes from his brief letter. J.B. Mayor writes that Jude is probably one of the youngest of the brothers of Jesus. He writes that Jude was married and accompanied by his wife on missionary journeys. Mayor believes Jude wrote his letter many years after his brother's death and supplied additional warnings about the perilous circumstances of the new age. Mayor concludes that Jude's letter is written after the letter of James as Jude is familiar with the writings of Paul. Such expressions as "most holy faith" and "tradition once delivered to the saints," reinforce this belief. Mayor believes that difficulties of mentioning the destruction of Jerusalem are resolved if the date of this letter is near 80 A.D.[37]

Family relationships in the New Testament are extremely complex. James was a very common name as was Mary, John, and Judah or Jude. During the ministry of Jesus, Jude is one of the unbelievers (John 7:5). When writing his letter, Jude makes two significant claims: he is a servant of Jesus Christ, and he is a brother of James. Jude recognizes the prominence of his brother James. However, both James and Jude display humility, perhaps not wanting to broadcast their relationship to Jesus. Jude's writing has similar wording as his brother James. Jude relies heavily upon Old Testament sources, and he is extremely interested in the faithful practices of the early Christians.

Jude seems to be more associated with the concerns of Peter regarding the Apocalypse than James. By the time of Jude's letter, the term *a common salvation* is present, and the letter of Jude is placed towards the end of the biblical canon; only the Apocalypse of John follows.

Both James and Jude are concerned with Christians of Jewish background, although both brothers recognize that racial and ethnic barriers have no place in Christianity. Both recognize Jesus their brother as "The Lord Jesus Christ." Both realize the coming parousia of Jesus Christ: "The Lord will soon be here" (James 5:8); "And keep in step with God's love. As you wait for our Lord Jesus Christ to show how kind he is by giving you eternal life" (Jude 21). There is no doubt Jude uses Jewish writings to support his letter, including such writings as the prophecies of Enoch: "The Lord is coming with thousands and thousands of holy angels to judge everyone" (Jude 14–15). Jude also mentions Michael, the Archangel, and his struggle with Satan (Jude 9).

Both James and Jude are extremely concerned with righteous conduct, and both brothers see Jesus Christ as a loving and forgiving savior. A careful reading of both letters shows the Jewish heritage of the brothers, very similar to that of Jesus Christ. James seems to be the more practical of the two; Jude delves into ancient sources and appears more esoteric in his viewpoint. Together the brothers capture some of the paradoxical wisdom of their earthly brother and eternal Lord and Savior, Jesus Christ.

CHAPTER 4

JAMES AND JOHN, THE SONS OF ZEBEDEE

James and His Brother John

The Expositor's Greek Testament poses another interesting family tie in the life of Jesus. "If Salome was Mary's sister, then Jesus and John were cousins."[38] James and John are always listed as brothers, the sons of Zebedee, in the gospel writings. Their mother is pictured as an assertive woman always wanting what she thinks will advance her sons in the kingdom of Jesus.

James and John are very early on described as young fishermen working with their father, Zebedee (Matthew 4:21). They are certainly what the modern world would call "middle class." Their father remains an obscure tradesman, but their mother has a slightly different persona in the gospel writings. Matthew records an interesting intervention by their mother. She boldly asks Jesus to promote her sons above the other disciples of Jesus. The other disciples are obviously upset, but Jesus defuses the situation with a wonderful lesson on the nature of greatness (Matthew 20:20-28). Mark also mentions their grab for power but chooses to leave out the mother's part. However, Mark is the only writer to reveal her name as "Salome" and place her at the crucifixion (Mark 15:40).

Matthew 10:2 mentions John, and, as usual, his brother James receives the prominence as the son of Zebedee, with John listed as James's brother. Probably at this time Matthew recognized John the Baptist as the John who is well-known. The Baptist was the great preacher, and Matthew elevates his standing to a list of prophets that includes Elijah and Jeremiah (Matthew 16:14). Further reading in Matthew shows the special relationship that Jesus has with the brothers, the sons of Zebedee. In Matthew 17: 11-13, Jesus takes the brothers with Simon Peter up to a high mountain where they witness the transfiguration of Jesus. All of them see Moses and Elijah revealed, and Peter offers to build tabernacles for the occasion. Even at this time of euphoria, John is relatively obscure and mentioned as the brother of James.

Matthew records another occasion when the brothers are in the private company of Jesus. At Gethsemane, Jesus takes Peter and the "two sons of Zebedee: into the deeper recesses of this garden where He was to spend many solemn hours in prayer. Unfortunately, these three disciples fell asleep and were no consolation to Him" (Matthew 26:36-46).

Mark and Luke document other references to these brothers that Matthew omits. Mark records that Jesus gave the brothers the name Boanerges or "Sons of Thunder" (Mark 3:17). Jesus understands that the brothers are short tempered. Many scholars have been quick to describe only Peter in this way. Mark also mentions the brothers, along with Jesus and Peter, going to the house of a ruler of a synagogue where the ruler's daughter was raised from death (Mark 5:35-43).

Luke states that James and John are Peter's partners in a fishing business (5:10). The Greek word *koinonoi* can be translated as people who share a common bond, such as these three fishermen.

The Maturity of the Apostle John

Luke is the writer who exposes the brothers as willing to burn down a village that would not accept Jesus (Luke 9:49-56). Much later in the ministry of Jesus, Luke details the story of the preparation that is assigned to Peter and John for the last Passover meal (Luke 27:7-13). This preparation task includes the arrangements for the upper room where all of the disciples later share their most intimate thoughts with Jesus. John is sent without James indicating that Jesus observes a growing maturity in the future apostle.

The treatment of John by the other gospel writers is an interesting mixture. He is shown to be volatile early on in the ministry and then responsible in the latter. John begins to create his own identity; he is not just the son of Zebedee or the brother of James, and although he is not the natural leader that Peter is, neither is John always reticent. Jesus sees in him an energy that bursts forward, sometimes with inappropriate zeal. John's character continues to be refined. F.F. Bruce states that in the year 44 A.D. Judea and Galilee become joined as the one province of Judea. Bruce emphasizes that only in that year did Galilee become part of Judea and "so directly subject to imperial rule." This is also the year that Herod Agrippa and James, the brother of John die. Luke records both deaths in the Book of Acts.[39]

External forces are pressing on John, the other son of Zebedee. The loss of his brother would have created a great trauma, yet he does not record this tragedy in his writings. The Jewish Zealot party would have been completely opposed to the consolidation of Roman rule in Israel. The church in Jerusalem would also feel the pressure of persecution. Herod Agrippa, before his death in the year 44 A.D., considers the growth of the church to be a threat. The influx of believers as recorded in chapter two of Acts, and the merger of Hebraistic and Hellenistic Jews as recorded in the sixth chapter of Acts, distress local Jewish religious leaders who partner with Herod Agrippa to halt such growth. Hence the execution of James is ordered. Persecution against evangelists increases and, in one case in Acts, leads to death. The martyr-dom of Stephen reinforces that the church is undergoing intense pressure. However, out of this pressure, a preaching partnership is formed.

In Acts 3:1, the announcement is made of the preaching partner-ship consisting of Peter and John: "Now Peter and John went up together to the temple at the hour of prayer." Notice how far John has traveled spiritually from being just the other brother or one of the sons of Zebedee. Great change has occurred since the fiery "Son of Thunder" wanted to eliminate the opponents of Jesus. When Peter and John become preaching partners, Luke writes in Acts 4:13 that these men are "uneducated and untrained filling the leaders with amazement." Many modern sermons have been preached about these comments to prove that Peter and John are little more than country bumpkins unable to complete or write a sentence. While it is certainly true that their lives were filled with the Holy Spirit, Peter and John are quite well-educated for their time and position. Bruce comments that "illiterate" was not the intended meaning of "uneducated" in this verse. He rath-er emphasizes that Peter and John are working class people or businessmen. The conclusion can only be that Peter and John are teaching with authority, and that God is using the power of two intelligent, spirit-filled men to exercise His will in Jerusalem.[40]

It can be noticed that where Peter is the spokesman in the earlier chapters, Luke later records both men speaking with undaunted courage. "Whether it is right in the sight of God to listen to you more than to God, you judge. For we cannot but speak the things which we have seen and heard" (Acts 4:19-20). The transformation in John's life is complete. There is no turning back. His heart had already been without fear, and now his tongue expresses his wit-ness for the Christ. Still, John is not considered the leader of the Jerusalem church. Luke records Peter as arbiter and spokesman in the Ananias and Sapphira scandal recorded in the fifth chapter of Acts. In the sixth chapter of Acts, Peter and the apostles delegate the Hellenistic widow problems to a number of special servants. Among those servants is Stephen who, as previously mentioned, becomes a martyr for Christ. Philip is one of the servants, and he later preaches and converts the Ethiopian noble.

In Acts 12, Luke focuses on the trials and tribulations of Peter. John is absent from this story. The death of his brother James by execution must have weighed heavily upon him. John does appear at the Jerusalem conference in the year 50 A.D. Luke records the events of the conference in Acts 15. The apostle Paul in his letter to the Galatians refers to Peter and John as "pillars" in the Jerusalem church (Galatians 2).

During these years after 50 A.D. John, in all probability, remains in Jerusalem. As far as can be known, the Jerusalem church is unable to assist Paul when he is a prisoner in Caesarea. Paul does not receive a visit from Peter, John, or James, the Lord's brother, during this time, according to the scriptural record. The reason might have been avoiding persecution, but the fact remains that Paul and the Jerusalem church have little partnership during this period.

The condition of the Jerusalem church remains much in question even after the relief effort from other churches. Demographics are rapidly changing. Eusebius, a leading church historian, observes that the apostles in Jerusalem, being "harassed in innumerable ways, with a view to destroy them, and driven from the land of Judea, had gone forth to preach the gospel to all nations, relying on the aid of Christ."[41] Eusebius writes at length about the terrible sufferings of those Christians remaining in Jerusalem and mentions those who flee to a city called Pella beyond the Jordan. Are Peter and John in this group? Again no documented record exists that confirms either Peter or John are still in the Jerusalem area in the 60s or at the time of the destruction of the Temple in 70 A.D. Conclusions can be drawn that during those years John matures into a respected evangelist, having changed his attitudes toward Gentiles. Yet, he is still not the leader that Peter, Paul, or James, the brother of Jesus, have become. John is a stable member of the Jerusalem church, indeed one of the pillars, but his greatest years lay ahead in the city of Ephesus.

CHAPTER 4

THE FAMILY OF JESUS CHRIST

Tradition in the first century church is almost unanimous in stating that John, son of Zebedee, moves to Ephesus in his later years. The earliest years of Christianity demonstrate different viewpoints towards evangelism. Peter, John, and James, the brother of Jesus, stay in the area of Jerusalem. On the other hand, men like Paul begin their trips to the Gentile world beginning in the 40s and continuing those trips even after the fall of Jerusalem in 70 A.D.

James becomes the great moderator in the Jerusalem church, even more than Peter. Paul and James help broker a great compromise in the year 50 A.D. at Jerusalem. John is witness to the events of this meeting, but he maintains a fondness for teaching Jewish brethren, as does Peter and James. Also, John may have been caring for the mother of Jesus. Does John continue to be Mary's caretaker, or does Jesus' brother James and other family members become more involved? These questions are not answered in the scriptures. There can be little doubt that John gains from Mary even more insight into the life of Jesus, for John's writings reflect that insight.

John spends his final years in the great city of Ephesus according to tradition. His death occurs around 100 A.D. We can also project that John, as well as Peter, leaves Jerusalem before the year 70 A.D. Tradition speculates that Mary may have died in Jerusalem. However, other tradition indicates that she died in Ephesus. John, although reared in a small town, becomes a city dweller. Wayne Meeks, a noted church historian, writes that "Paul was a city person."[42] The same could eventually be said about John.

In Ephesus John becomes the respected "elder" and there most likely writes his gospel and letters. John had been schooled in the Greek language, as are all Jewish artisans and businessmen. J.W. Roberts, in his commentary of James, observes that it is well known "that there was a deep penetration of Greek influence affecting Galilee especially."[43]

The Gospel of John

The first book associated with John is his gospel. In his commentary, Frank Pack makes the statement that it is unanimous among the scholars of the late second century that "John, brother of James and son of Zebedee, wrote the gospel in his old age while living at Ephesus." Pack notes that the internal evidence of this gospel overwhelmingly points to John the Apostle as the writer. This includes a multitude of details that only an eyewitness could know, including the geography and topography of Israel; the attitude of the Jewish male population toward women; the times and specific locations of feasts; the weariness of Jesus at the well of Jacob; the five loaves in the multiplication miracle being identified as barley loaves; the number of water pots in the house at Cana given as six; the number of fish (153) caught by the disciples when Jesus prepared breakfast on the shore; and the identification by name of the high priest's servant whose ear Peter cut off. Pack concludes that these details and many others "come from one who saw and bore witness to them."[44]

The question arises, why another gospel? The so-called synoptic gospels had been written. Was the story of Jesus not completely told? According to John, there is a need for a special story about Jesus from not only an eyewitness, but from one who had a unique perspective. "The Word became flesh and dwelt among us, and we beheld his glory, the glory as of the only begotten of the Father, full of grace and truth" (John 1:14). From a passage like this the reader immediately can notice that the Gospel of John is different. The stories are different in content with much more detail. There is a great emphasis on the last days of the life of Jesus.

Then there is the word transliterated "logos." The use of the Greek word "logos" has been the object of intensive and exhaustive research. Pack suggested that the use of "logos" is an attention getter for "Hellenistic Greek readers."[45] "Logos" can be translated in English as "reason" or "logic." The main thrust of John's opening words or prologue examines the difficult concept of the immortal becoming mortal, the eternal creator living with the created.

CHAPTER 4

To John this means life overcoming death, and light dispelling darkness.

We have, by John's account, the eternal deity living among the darkness of this world and spreading the holy light of His presence. No more profound passage of scripture exists. The Word becomes flesh and becomes the rationale for our faith and our hope. John's opening verses introduce us to an eternal world.

John, more than any other gospel writer, concentrates on the dialogues of Jesus. Three of these dialogues or lengthy conversations are in the opening chapters. John remembers a certain wedding feast at Cana, near Nazareth, where he is present with Jesus, the disciples, and the mother of Jesus. This is the most personal of the conversations since family members are involved. John is surely a witness and probably obtains details from Mary herself. Since these Jewish weddings last for days, disasters could happen. John remembers that when Jesus considers the predicament of the wine, he somewhat reluctantly remedies the situation with His first miracle (John 2:1-12). Jesus performs miracles only when there is a special need and certainly not at every distressful situation. He is very unlike the public charlatans of that day or of more modern times who exploit the helpless. Jesus realizes that His ministry is not just one of miracles. He does not heal everyone or raise the dead in every village.

John remembers the first miracle of Jesus as the special request of Mary. This miracle demonstrates that Mary has already sensed the extraordinary power of her son. Jesus, she knows, is struggling with the use of that power. Is a lack of wine at a wedding feast a suitable crisis for the use of His might? John concludes that Mary knows Jesus is not only the healer of physical illness but the healer of social embarrassment. He is the Lord of healing and the source of joy. Jesus' human side is fully revealed at Cana when He sees the sadness and anxiety of the wedding party. John is able to record the details of the situation as no one else. Unfortunately the interpretation of this miracle has often concentrated on the alcoholic content of the wine, or on the seemingly harsh reply that Jesus makes to His mother. A focus such as these misses the depth of the story. The reason John records the miracle is because he wants the world to see Jesus as a man of compassion, and a man interested in the joy and everyday existence of others. The original language shows that Jesus does not speak disrespectfully to His mother. When He realizes that the time has come to demonstrate His power, He does so simply, with the knowledge of the servants, some of his family, and his disciples, but not in a moment of fanfare for the wedding guests (John 2:7-12).

Other lengthy dialogues are chosen by John for obvious reasons. Immediately, the reader can recognize the great contrast in the social standings of Nicodemus and the Samaritan woman who are the people Jesus chooses for the conversations recorded in the third and fourth chapters of John. Nicodemus and the Samaritan woman are poles apart: one the epitome of the orthodox, respected and at the top of the social strata—the other an outcast, racially and socially. Yet, John sees that both of them have a great desire for truth while harboring major deficiencies in their understanding of the Messiah.

In the third chapter, John describes Nicodemus as one of the rulers of the Jews. He comes to hear Jesus by night, perhaps for his own safety as well as for the safety of Jesus. Nicodemus has concluded that Jesus is a teacher from God and recognizes that Jesus can also perform miracles through the power of God. During their conversation, Jesus seizes the opportunity to reveal the concept of spiritual rebirth. Jesus answers the question of Nicodemus, "How can a man be born when he is old?" (John 3:4), by answering that the birth is of water and spirit.

Westcott writes in his commentary that water and spirit are part of the cosmic balance of the outward and the inward. He adds that Christian baptism in our own era fulfills the outward act of faith while the birth of the spirit seals as well as unites this outward act. The concept of the Spirit's action on the believer is compared to the mysterious ways of the wind. Westcott suggests that the believer by word and deed validates that an invisible influence has inspired and moved him.[46] Nicodemus finally admits that he cannot understand such teachings (John 3:9). As a symbol of the old order and the status quo, he cannot grasp the new order of things. Still, his world has been turned upside down by Jesus.

Nicodemus believes that Jesus is a great teacher, but then Jesus tells him that He has been sent to earth as the unique Son of Man. Could Nicodemus believe this about Jesus? As F.L. Godet in his commentary stresses, the Son of Man becomes the sole revealer of divine things, and Nicodemus is allowed to glimpse the heavenly secrets. Among these great secrets, is the universal love of God through Christ. Nicodemus had not foreseen such revelations when he made a nightly appointment to visit Jesus. He comes knowing that Jesus is a remarkable teacher, but now he has been introduced to this teacher as the Savior of the World. Nicodemus now realizes that he must experience a most radical change in his life. He can no longer regard Jesus as just another Godly teacher. For this mature Pharisee, the night has become day, and the old has been replaced by the new.[47]

John chooses another personal dialogue to share a scene from Samaria. One can conclude that, again in this instance, John is a witness as he is at Cana. This scene is quite different from the encounter with Nicodemus. As Luke drew the deep contrast in the Good Samaritan and the religious leaders, so John is saying that both the religious leaders and the outcasts of society need Jesus.

The dialogue with the Samaritan woman begins on a piece of land in Samaria near the traditional site of Jacob's well. In this remote area, Jesus sees none of the amenities of Hellenistic civilization. During this period of time the Roman world is replete with examples of this civilization as exhibited by the building programs started by Augustus and carried on by Tiberius.

In such ruins as Pompeii, one is provided with a time capsule of first century Roman life. At Pompeii, the remains of the theatre, the palestra, the baths, the homes, and the basilica still exist. As the archaeologist Salvatore Nappo observes, "Even the problems of the water supply were solved by the great aqueduct."[48] In Israel, Caesarea Maritime provided similar luxuries of the Roman kind. But at the well of Jacob, Jesus is far away from the civilized world.

John, who is probably living in Ephesus as he writes his gospel account, is far removed from Jacob's well. In Ephesus John lives near the huge temple of Artemis that is described by the historian Wayne Meeks as "one of the seven wonders of the world."[49] Even to the Jewish population of the first century, Samaria is considered the very dregs of the inhabited world. Perhaps only the wild province of Bithynia could be worse. Jacob's well has been described by the scholar Jerome Murphy-O'Connor as "a deep well thirty five meters near Nablus."[50] In later years, about 380 A.D., a church is built on this site. The crusaders find the place to be a strategic location and build a new church on the same site in the twelfth century. Steven Runciman, the noted medieval scholar, records that Queen Melisandre lives in this region from 1152-1161 A.D. and that, as she grows older, she becomes "interested in pious works. She was known to found religious houses on a generous scale throughout her widowhood and made several grants of land to the church of the Holy Sepulcher in Jerusalem."[51]

In John the Apostle's time, Jesus is dealing with Samaritan people who have some identity with the patriarch Jacob and who are considered vastly inferior by the Judeans and Galileans. When Jesus meets the Samaritan woman, she is very surprised to see a Jewish male ready to converse with her. Unlike Nicodemus, who values his position as a religious leader and comes to Jesus by night, this woman is forced by her own society to come to the well in the middle of the day with its searing heat. This contrast of meeting time is emphasized by John (3:2; 4:6).

Jesus creates détente immediately when He asks her for water from the well. This seems a simple request by most standards, but by the mores of that time and place, the request is a complete surprise to the woman. Such hatred exists between Jews and

Samaritans that the woman is wary and says, "You are a Jew and I am a Samaritan woman. How can you ask me for a drink?" (John 4:9).

John recognizes later, perhaps by talking to the woman herself, that Jesus uses this opportunity to move from the necessities of this life to the eternal verities. He tells her about the gift of God and who is able to grant it to her. The gift of living water is discussed. The woman seems to be theologically puzzled as was Nicodemus, who answers Jesus with a hint of skepticism. Is it confusion, disbelief, or a light brushing off when she asks Jesus, "Give me this water so that I won't get thirsty and have to keep coming here to draw water" (John 4:15)? Her tone is not clear, but the conversation continues.

After more exchanges in which Jesus reveals the secrets of her personal life (five husbands and a live-in boyfriend), the woman acknowledges that He indeed is a prophet (John 4:19). Perhaps to divert the discussion from her love life, she changes the subject to a question about places of worship, a topic as important in ancient times as it is in the modern world. As with Nicodemus, Jesus explains the new order of religious life, the spirit and truth concept. Then He chooses the outcast woman of Samaria to make his great pronouncement that He is the Messiah (4:26). As Pack concludes, "to the Samaritan woman Jesus claimed first from his own life to be the promised Messiah for Samaritans, for Jews, and for all men."[52]

In addition to his highlighting these important conversations, John also places special emphasis on specific miracles of Jesus. The healing of the paralyzed man at the pool of Bethsaida re-inforces the concept of compassion in His miracles. John sees Jesus heal an obviously disabled person who had been ill for thirty-eight years. John records in detail these years of illness, the inability of the man to reach the healing waters before the others, and the complaints of the religious leaders who want no healing on the Sabbath (John 5:1-18). The point is clear to John: neither God the Father, nor the Son Jesus, rest from doing good works.

As in the dialogues, Jesus is proclaiming a new order of life unfettered by the traditions of the past.

The healing of the blind man recorded in John 9 is John's natural progression into the complexity of the miracle process. The question is raised by his disciples as to who sinned to cause this man's blindness (9:1). Pack enlightens us when he comments, "The rabbis held that the child could sin in the mother's womb. When a pregnant woman worshipped in a pagan temple, the unborn child also worshipped the idol. Also they held that the sins of the parents might be the reason for affliction."[53] Against such religious traditions, still to some degree present in more recent times, Jesus performs this miracle. John quickly realizes that something is happening greater than the healing of physical sight. Jesus takes on the great task of healing *spiritual blindness*, always present in any age. He has come to wipe away the darkness of prejudice, misconception, and tradition. The blind man sees more than his critics and pronounces that Jesus is from God. "If this man were not from God, he could do nothing" (John 9:33). John sadly sees that the healed man's reward for such perception is excommunication from the synagogue. The spiritual blindness of the world around him remains, and the spiritual leaders see least of all.

John records one miracle that stands on its own as both the greatest sign of the resurrection power of Jesus and also the most tender of healing encounters. The story of His friend Lazarus has been simply called the "resurrection miracle." John recalls miracles relieving hunger and miracles relieving the suffering of the body. In the eleventh chapter, John presents the greatest of all the miracles of Jesus: one that presents His power over even death.

The family of Lazarus is very special to both Jesus and John. Their friendship is of the closest nature, and on several occasions this family provides Jesus and the disciples with an earthly home. Oddly, we have little knowledge of the family itself. Only John of the gospel writers mentions Lazarus. Luke mentions the sisters, Mary and Martha, while showing their contrasting personalities. Mary is pictured as the intuitive one whom John admires. Martha is more pragmatic, busy with the order of the home (Luke 10:38-42). John describes Lazarus in these words, "Now Jesus loved Martha and his sister and Lazarus" (11:5).

The story simply told describes Lazarus as very ill. Jesus seems to delay going to him, and finally Lazarus dies. Jesus then travels to the family's home in Bethany where both sisters speak freely to Jesus and tell Him that their brother would not have died if He had come to Bethany sooner (John 11:1-33).

John, in recalling this story in later years, sees the plan that Jesus had for the situation. He would raise Lazarus from the dead four days after his death. As Jewish tradition observes, by the fourth day, the soul had ample time to leave the body. Both Martha and Mary recognize the extraordinary healing power of Jesus, but neither grasp His control of life and death. Perhaps they are not quite sure about the other raisings from the dead since they were done quickly after the person's death. Both sisters were grieving with a sense of hopelessness. All of this, especially the sight of the vulnerable Mary, moves Jesus to His most caring moment in the gospel: her genuine lament, as well as the lament of others, moves him to tears (John 11:35). John at this point, above all the other gospel writers, merges the divine with the human in Christ.

This miracle also displays to John the complete submission of Jesus to the Father God. As Paul writes in the Philippian letter, Jesus, even though of equal nature and stature with the Father, lives on earth as a dutiful servant with complete submission to the Father. In this miracle, Jesus thanks His Father for hearing His prayer and allowing Him to demonstrate the glory of the one true God (John 11:41-42). Humility and submission are rare commodities in the religious world of that time as well as today. When Jesus has those standing at the tomb of Lazarus remove the stone, he shows mankind's proper submission to God's power. The resurrection of Lazarus is then completed with few additional signs. A loud voice is sufficient (11:43). John once again shows the simple way in which Jesus demonstrates the power of God. The completion of this miracle foretells the death of Jesus. From that moment on, He is considered a great danger to the religious authorities as well as the Roman government. John says that Jesus no longer travels openly (John 11:54). Six days before Passover, He dines with the resurrected Lazarus for the last time (John 12:1).

John does not use parables as the other gospel writers. He does use the metaphors and models which Jesus left. As a close observer, John records many scenes such as the anointing of Jesus at Bethany by Mary after the resurrection of her brother. The timing is spectacular. Lazarus is present at the dinner. Jesus is there in Bethany, the town that was so dear to Him. The closest friends of this special family are there. Martha, as usual, is serving as hostess. Mary realizes her complete devotion to her Lord. The identity of Mary cannot be in dispute. John, in his careful way, makes a point to mention Lazarus and Martha. Only Mary, their sister who lived in Bethany, fit the profile of complete devotion. When Mary anoints the body of Jesus with an expensive ointment, she knows this is the proper thing to do. Marcus Dods in his commentary writes, "This anointing was his true embalming. Mary's love was representative of the love of his intimate friends in whose loyal affection he was embalmed so that his memory could never die. The significance of the incident lies precisely in this, that Mary's action is the evidence that Jesus may now die, having already found an enduring place for himself in the regard of his friends."[54]

Mary's act of supreme devotion is significant to John because she blends the logical with the spontaneous. She must have calculated both the cost of the ointment and the time for the anointing. When she washes the feet of Jesus and dries them with her hair, John sees an act of incomparable love and devotion. The act of unbinding the hair is not usually done by a Jewish woman in public. In a true sense, she is unbinding her soul. How great is her devotion in contrast to the negative comments of those at the dinner. Judas Iscariot is one who camouflages his greed by criticizing the act as wasteful. Yet Jesus knows that Judas has impure motives while Mary is pure in heart (John 12:1-10). In John 13 the writer presents his Lord as the model of service. John records events that have the most profound influence on him in later years. At this point he recalls an event that occurs during Passover week. Pack translates the pivotal verse in the present tense as the context dictates. Jesus rises from the table, lays aside His garments, and wraps a towel around Him. Then He pours water into a basin and begins the process of washing the disciples' feet. The present tense emphasizes that John could not forget the scene even many years later. The concept of service in rabbinic teaching never goes to this extreme. Yet Jesus is always doing the unusual, touching the leper, exorcizing the demonized, eating with the tax collector, forgiving the sinful woman. Rabbinic teaching does not require even a Jewish slave to wash feet.[55]

Jesus has to tell Peter in a candid manner that He will have no part of him if Peter will not let Him wash his feet. Peter then consents, although he does not see the double meaning of cleansing (John 13:8). Jesus is foretelling His own sacrificial cleansing on the cross with His blood. He is also giving His disciples an example of life in service. John 13:14-15 is climactic: "If I then, your Lord and Teacher, have washed your feet, you also ought to wash one another's feet. For I have given you an example that you should do as I have done to you." Pack interprets, "Jesus had given them a supreme example (*hupodeigma*), that applied to all their relationships to one another. The example of Jesus in this as in so many other things has been a most powerful incentive for devoted, sacrificial living and service among his followers."[56]

Another model of life is portrayed by John in the seventeenth chapter. Jesus is shown praying His own prayer. This prayer is in reality the Lord's Prayer. After reading the prayer that John remembers, a three-part division can be seen.

1. Jesus asks for His own glorification. In a cosmic sense Christ is following His own admonition to ask, seek, and knock. As in all of the requests of Jesus, He thinks of His followers. He desires to give the ultimate gift, eternal life. John refers to eternal life in John 17:3 as knowledge of the only true God and His son Jesus Christ. In this case

knowledge is more than rational consent but a complete bonding with God. The scholar Westcott comments, "It is not an acquaintance with facts as external, nor an intellectual conviction of their reality, but an apprehension of the truth by the whole nature of man."[57]

2. Jesus prays for His followers to be protected. He is facing His own greatest crisis, but He thinks of those who will be left. John has many years of life for which to be thankful. Perhaps in his later years he remembers, "Holy Father keep through thine own name those whom thou hast given me that they may be one as we are" (John 17:11).

3. Protection comes from God, but the third part of the prayer is a choice made by each follower of Jesus. Many have concluded that this prayer of Jesus is a call for unity. Certainly unity is a great consideration of Jesus, but protection from evil is an equal concern. John has lived long enough to know that the Evil One enters the heart of Christians to cause division. In a seeming contradiction of language, Jesus requests that His disciples not remain cloistered from the world, but at the same time, not participate in the world's beliefs. John knows the dangers of reclusive righteousness as well as the pitfalls of moral compromise. He never backs down from his beliefs from the time he is a young evangelist through the persecutions of the Emperor Domitian.

John can see that the prayer answered the requests for protection and unity by a call for a consecration of soul and a cleansing of spirit. This complete consecration can only be accomplished by adherence to truth. Truth here represents the full spectrum of God's revelations to humanity. These revelations are shown through natural forces of creation, revelations from the prophets of old, and finally through His Son. Westcott simply describes it as "the sum of the Christian revelation."[58]

CHAPTER 4

Jesus is truly praying for future generations. Many times the prayer has been used to implore unity of faith, but often the concluding verse has been forgotten, "and I have declared unto them thy name, and will declare it: that the love wherewith thou hast loved me may be in them, and I in them" (John 17:26). The definition of unity in these concluding words of the prayer has been interpreted in various ways.

- Pack writes, "One of the strongest arguments confronting the world is the unity of Christ's followers based on his word." [59]

- Westcott expands this unity in an almost esoteric aura, "Some mysterious mode which we cannot distinctly apprehend, a vital unity. In this sense it is the gospel of a higher type of life, in which each constituent being is a conscious element in the being of a vast whole." [60]

Both commentators are correct. Unity of believers has been based on the words of our Father. However, unity can never be achieved unless love is present. The divisiveness of the religious world has always had elements of contempt and bigotry. In the Middle Ages, crusading efforts often included massacre and pillage. The conquest of Jerusalem in 1099 by the crusaders was savage. Islamic forces then retaliated. Runciman's history of the crusades is filled with acts of brutality done in the name of religion. [61] Can anyone believe that Jesus prayed for such atrocities? Rather He prayed that the fellowship of believers be demonstrated by love, the love of the Father for the Son, and the transmission of that love to all believers. Thus, the very personal prayer of Jesus ends. It is a prayer as intense as any with the exception of the prayer in the Garden of Gethsemane. Certainly, it has been a prayer for all the ages. The themes have continued to be universal in nature. John remembers this prayer, has pondered its contents all of his life, and reveals its glorious message for future generations.

John is the gospel writer who uses many metaphors. In the picture of the good shepherd in John 10, Jesus tells a familiar story to

His listeners. He chooses an occupation that is ordinary but familiar in the ancient world. The Jewish people could recall many good shepherds among their ancestors. Abraham had many flocks and herds. Beloved David spent his youth watching over his father's herds. Jesus may have had such illustrious shepherds in mind when He emphasizes that the good shepherd will defend his sheep even to the point of risking his life. Abraham was forced into battle over his flocks, and David defended his sheep from wild animals. The key word is "ownership." The good shepherd is not just doing his job, but he possesses the sheep and would never flee from them.

In a similar sense John is saying that Jesus owns us, body and soul. The ownership is not referring to natural possession but a personal relationship. John knows at this later time in history that Jesus, as the shepherd, not only leads us but protects us. John sees the great mass of believers as other sheep, and the message of Christ's love and protection penetrates all barriers and extends throughout all generations. John described the story as a *paroimia*, a story similar to a parable, but with more of the mysterious. In any case the disciples do not understand the message any more easily than the more common parable. Jesus adds to the metaphorical language by asserting that He is also the door through which the sheep enter safely.

In returning to the thoughts of David in Psalm 23, Jesus becomes the fulfillment of the Lord as Shepherd. He becomes forever the provider for the needs of His disciples. He continuously sets the table for His followers. He destroys the fear of evil and accompanies His flock through the dangerous valleys. Goodness and mercy follow His own people, and they enjoy His company always.

In chapter 15, John provides an even more intimate metaphor. Here Jesus refers to Himself as the vine and the disciples as the branches. Again as with the sheep, Jesus chooses a most familiar scene. Then as now vineyards stretched from the Mount Carmel region down through Bethshemesh and the land of Samson. As one gazes at the vineyards with the grapes planted close to the

CHAPTER 4

ground, one is reminded that a traveler in Israel cannot miss the beautiful imagery of the vineyard. Pack states that Israel is a land of vineyards, and the vine is associated with the "life of the people." [62]

John's emphasis in this metaphor is clearly the productive Christian life. However, that production cannot be separated from the Christian's connection with the source of all strength and beauty, Jesus Christ. Some interpretations associate the vine symbol with communion, but Jesus might not have had this specifically in mind. Certainly the Lord's Supper later becomes the ultimate symbol of the vine as well as the bread, but the imagery can stand apart from this reference. This metaphor represents God, the Father, as the vine dresser. As Israel is the vine in the Old Testament, Jesus and His Father play these roles in the New Testament. God becomes the overseer. The productive branches of the vineyard are praised and become one with Christ. The unproductive ones are thrown away. When Paul writes about the fruit of the spirit, he is using a similar metaphor.

This metaphor extends the concept of the Christian's total reliance on Christ, not in the sense of protection as in the Good Shepherd, but in the realm of good works. Good works for the Christian are not a way to attach to Christ but rather are produced from the connection that is already there. We have become bearers of good works through our total commitment to the grace shown by God (Ephesians 2: 8-10). We did not create ourselves as branches in the vineyard but will grow and become fruitful through our love for Christ.

Another appealing metaphor that John relates is, without question, the most intimate of all. John contrasts the bread of life with the manna of the Old Testament (John 6:32-33). Again this passage has often been used in connection with communion, but John is obviously thinking far beyond that subject. To His audience Jesus presents His most radical teaching. To those who listen, the whole discourse about flesh and blood qualifies as one of His hard or difficult sayings. John points out several eternal promises that his Lord makes to those who would eat and drink.

- The cessation of spiritual hunger and thirst could be accomplished (6:35). John sees about him a deplorable spiritual famine. Only Jesus can provide spiritual nourishment.

- Jesus also promises acceptance to all those who come to Him (6:40). How different from the message of exclusion that so many are hearing.

- Also, Jesus promises to become an inward part of all people who are willing to put their trust in Him (6:41-68). How similar were His words to Paul's proclamation that Christ lives within each Christian?

Westcott states that the key verse of the chapter is verse 51, "I am the living bread that came down from heaven. Whoever eats this bread will live forever. This bread is my flesh, which I will give for the life of the world," which is fulfilled in Christ's incarnation and resurrection. "By his incarnation and resurrection the ruin and death which sin brought in are overcome. The close of the earthly life, the end of the life which is, in one aspect, of self for self, opens wider relations of life." [63]

Throughout the metaphor Jesus alludes to the Old Testament, in this case the manna of the wilderness wanderings. As in other comparisons, Jesus is pictured as the true and eternal, and the former is pictured as temporal. Manna sustains the people of Israel for only a brief period. It is a gift from heaven, and John does not discount that this bread is beneficial. John does point out that manna is not the eternal bread of life. Only Jesus provides the true (*alethes*) solution. As bread and drink are vital to this life, Jesus is our spiritual bread and drink for the eternal life. The expansion of this metaphor comes easily in the early church. The communion of bread and the fruit of the vine become

CHAPTER 4

integral in worship and serve as a reminder to the participants of John's account where he witnessed the true Bread of Life.

For John the defining period of time in his gospel is the last week of Christ's life on earth. More than any other gospel writer, he devotes his account to those last hours. Of all the gospel writers, only he witnesses the last supper, the farewells of service and prayer, the metaphor of the vine and branches, the betrayal, the trial, the crucifixion, and the resurrection. From chapters 13 through 21, John is our eyewitness, revealing to us the innermost secrets of Jesus.

After the Lord's Prayer of protection and unity, John carries us to the dark recesses of the Gethsemane Garden of the Kidron Valley. As one views the peaceful landscape today and the lush vegetation of the garden, one can hardly picture that dreadful scene found in John 18. Only John identifies the man that Peter attempts to kill with his sword while defending Jesus. John contrasts the old order with the new as Jesus willingly sacrifices Himself while Peter fights. Jesus shows to the world the submissive nature that He demonstrates even to the cross. John describes the scene as one of total subjection of Jesus to the will of God, the Father, as He drinks the cup that the Father has given Him. James Orr, in his article "Jesus Christ" contained in *The International Standard Bible Encyclopedia*, pictures the agony of Christ going beyond the horrible physical suffering to the realization of His dying for the sins of humanity.[64] John, who himself at times shows the explosive reaction similar to Peter, realizes that one must not use the sword. Paul mentions the submissive nature of Christ in the kenosis passage of Philippians 2 where Jesus empties himself of everything and becomes obedient even to "death on a cross" (Philippians 2:8).

After the events in the garden, John quickly turns to the trial of Jesus. The inquisition before Annas and Caiaphas reveals a little known part of John's life. John and Peter follow Jesus to the palace of the high priest (John 18:15). However, only John enters the palace with Jesus. John describes himself as the disciple who is known to the high priest as Peter stands outside in the court-yard (John 18: 15, 16). Westcott is aware of the tradition that John is privileged to wear the petalon, the plate attached to the high priest's headdress, the mitre.[65] Thus, we can conclude that John, of all the disciples, has the credentials to enter the venue of the trial and report on the proceedings. Pack interprets more when he recalls that early church tradition held that when John "was not at the temple serving as priest, he worked as a fisherman, and that John's family supplied fish for the high priest."[66]

The prestige of John's position allows him to witness the tragic denial by Peter of Jesus in the courtyard. John identifies one of the accusers of Peter as a "maid who kept the door" (John 18: 17). Godet reminds us that the "Hebrews very commonly had female doorkeepers."[67] Luke records the young girl who answers the door when Peter comes to the house of John Mark (Acts: 12). John adds to the validity of his witness when he recalls the charcoal fire that the servants had made (literally a heap of burning coals from which the English word "anthracite" comes). John uses the same word when he later describes the coals over which Jesus cooks fish (John 21:9).

John contrasts the drama of the examination of Jesus with the equally sad spectacle of Peter's denial. John, who must have known some of the priestly household, identifies one of Peter's questioners as a "kinsman of the man whose ear Peter had cut off" (John 18:26). John is also keenly aware of Jewish customs regarding Gentile courts. We can surmise that John fills the void left by other gospel writers in examining that Roman enigmatic figure, Pontius Pilate. In the eighteenth chapter of John, he pictures Pilate as baffled by the whole business. After all he does not see any real civil unrest perpetrated by Jesus Christ. Pilate remarks, "Am I a Jew? Your own nation and the chief priests have handed you over to me; what have you done?" Later he issues his most controversial of statements, "What is Truth?" (18:38) In Pilate, John sees the great contrast in the spiritual government of Christ versus the cynical, pragmatic power of the Roman government.

CHAPTER 4

In his final exchange with Jesus, Pilate chooses to dismiss Him after he finds that Jesus is more concerned with eternal matters than His own life. At that point Pilate has entered into the political labyrinth of compromise. He offers to release a prisoner, suggesting Jesus. The angry mob frustrates this plan by choosing Barabbas the murderer instead (18:40). After more conversations with Jesus about earthly matters and heavenly concepts, Pilate presents Jesus to the accusers. The crowd accuses Pilate as not being a friend of Caesar (*Caesaris Amicus*). Pilate caves in to political expediency. Pack summarizes Pilate's position, "He might lose his governship, he might be summoned to account before the emperor himself, and even suffer exile and public disgrace."[68] John sees Pilate as the ultimate display of the political, earthly mind. The man, who tells the crowd that he can find nothing wrong with Jesus (John 19:4-6), joins the forces of evil.

John, of all the apostles, is the only one at the crucifixion. He documents four women at the site. He does not dwell on the arduous walk of Jesus on the Via Dolorosa. No doubt he is there, but perhaps even late in life the memories are too painful. John does concentrate on Jesus as the fulfillment of the Old Testament as witnessed by him and others at the cross. The placard above the cross is mentioned only by John (19:19). He realizes that Jesus represents sovereignty through suffering. The three languages are symbolic to John. Years later in writing his gospel, he comprehends that this crude sign is a symbol of all humanity. Why in particular does John mention the four women at the cross? They are a diverse group and representative of that inscription above the cross. There was a great contrast between the mother of Jesus and Mary of Magdala. The first is chosen from all women to be the mother of the Son of God. The other is a recent follower of Jesus without the pedigree of other followers. Yet, both recognize Jesus as Lord. John's mother is also present, and she has been identified as the sister of Mary, the mother of Jesus. Perhaps John sees in these women at the cross a courage that the men do not have. During the crucifixion, John is selected by Jesus to take care of Mary, his mother (19:26-27).

John, as always, is very careful to point out the human as well as the divine characteristics of Christ. He sees in these actions and sayings of Christ the fulfillment of prophecy such as the parting of His garments; the extreme thirst; the bowl of vinegar (19:23, 28-29). John's great attention to detail and his prodigious memory as he writes molds the account into the most personal of experiences. His own emotions would have churned as he sees the Lord suffer as a human in the most horrible manner.

John sees the great symbolism. After the death of Jesus, the soldiers must test for any sign of life. The piercing of the side of Jesus is an act of brutality that John witnesses. On reflection later, he recognizes that blood and water coming from the body are distinct symbols. Just as the inscription on the placard shows the world-wide validation of Christ's rule, the blood and water are complete symbols of His saving power. Westcott reminds us that for John blood "is the symbol of the natural life and so especially of life as sacrificed. Water is the symbol of the spiritual life; and Christ by dying provided for the outpouring of the Spirit."[69] John now understands the concept of the living water and the body and the blood that he describes in the third and the sixth chapters of the gospel. John summarizes the death of Jesus with his personal testimony: "And he that saw it bare record, and his record is true" (John 19:35). "A bone of him shall not be broken, and they shall look on him whom they pierced" (John 19:36-37).

The mood changes in the Gospel of John when he reaches the climax of his account. He pays very special attention to the burial of Jesus. Ralph Gower writes about the burial customs of the time saying, "the body was normally washed, wrapped loosely in a linen cloth, and carried to a burial place on a wooden stretcher. Burial could take place in a natural cave or an artificially made one. This was done for Jesus by two wealthy men."[70] John is verifying for all that the death of Jesus is real, and the burial must take place. *The Expositor's Greek Testament* places the validity of the death as John's priority even unto the piercing of the body. "It is not the phenomenon of the blood and water he so emphatically certifies, but the veritable death of Christ."[71]

CHAPTER 4

John describes two unlikely benefactors in the funeral arrangements. Joseph, who is of Arimathea, and Nicodemus prepare the body for burial. Both are members of the Sanhedrin, both are rich, especially Joseph, and both must have been profoundly changed by Jesus (19:38-42). Nicodemus is now bold in his faith in Christ. John must have reflected on the spiritual growth in this man since visiting Jesus at night. Joseph uses his influence and wealth to properly care for the body including the providing of a garden tomb. Again, *The Expositor's Greek Testament* states, "The Friday was so nearly at an end that they had not time to go to any distance, and therefore availed themselves of the neighboring tomb as a provisional, if not permanent place."[72]

One can almost sense the relief that John feels as these two noble men come with courage, much beyond the other disciples, to bury the Lord. John alone of the gospel writers remembers the exact weight of the spices used as well as the place of the tomb (19:38-42). Whether John assists in the preparation for burial is unknown, but he is aware of so many details that such is possible, even probable. John has just experienced the most trying time of his life, a period he doesn't forget even fifty years later. This period of time drains him emotionally and depresses him beyond words. After sharing the intensity of His death, he is ready to present the glorified Christ in His resurrection.

John remembers a woman who comes to the garden alone. The other Gospels mention women, but John features Mary Magdalene. Only she has the courage to come to the tomb, and she comes very early. The other Gospels indicate that other women come not too much later. Mary then has the boldness to report the empty tomb to the disciples. John could not help but notice the fortitude of the women in contrast to the seclusion of the men. He mentions that Mary knows where to find Peter (20:2). Westcott writes that she comes to a lodging place where Jesus' mother is staying.[73]

The details following her report are quintessential Johannine reporting. Ever the stickler for details, John documents the foot race to the tomb. He reaches the sepulcher first, but waits for his friend Peter. When John enters the empty tomb, his life changes forever (20:3-9). Westcott concludes that, at this point, he separates himself from the other disciples. The agony of the garden burial, the cruelty of the cross, and the mystical references to resurrection begin to make sense. John remembers the careful way in which the clothing is arranged. Nothing had been hurried. He sees the empty tomb and believes.[74]

When the resurrected Christ appears to the disciples, John quickly notices His physical and spiritual capabilities. This is the resurrection body. Jesus moves through closed doors and appears and disappears suddenly. Yet the resurrection body still contains traces of the human body. Jesus has fresh scars in His hands and His side. John's inclusion of the appearance to Thomas and his doubt is probably not so much for the benefit of the other disciples and certainly not to embarrass Thomas, but it is for future generations who were not there to see the resurrected Christ. John recalls the special blessing of Christ on "those who have not seen and yet believe" (John 20:29). He then adds a closing comment on his account: "Now Jesus did many other signs in the presence of the disciples which are not written in this book; but these were written that you may believe that Jesus is the Christ, the Son of God, and that believing you may have life in his name" (John 20:30-31).

The closing chapter of John relates a breakfast scene by the sea. Here John is obviously an eyewitness. The story takes the disciples back to their roots of fishing. After a fruitless night on the lake, the disciples think they hear a stranger call out to them. He tells them to cast out their nets on the other side with the results that the disciples are unable to haul in such a great quantity of fish (21:1-6). John shows his intuitive nature when he recognizes the stranger as Jesus. Peter, always impetuous, jumps into the water and swims to shore. John then describes what took place next. The disciples had been without hope. Now, they find Jesus cooking their breakfast, even asking them for a few of their fish. John remembers the total catch to be 153 (21:7-11).

CHAPTER 4

Above all the story is not about the fish, but the reconciliation of Jesus with Peter (21:15-24). To John, Peter becomes the bedrock of the early church because of this reconciliation and forgiveness of Christ. His friend from the early days on the Sea of Galilee is now transformed into the leader of the Lord's church. John closes his message in triumph. Jesus has prevailed over death, and now Peter has overcome his fears.

John has many years to ponder his own role. Why would he be the last of the twelve? As we look back through the centuries, we can see that John, of all the followers, is given the spiritual insight and sensitivity to write such a gospel. He alone can adequately describe the Word becoming flesh, Who lived, grew tired and thirsty, even cooked a morning meal for a group of men who had all but given up hope and purpose. John changes from a son of thunder to a blessed apostle.

The First Letter of John

> That which was from the beginning, which we have heard, which we have seen with our eyes, which we have looked upon, and our hands have handled, of the Word of life; For the life was manifested, and we have seen it, and bear witness, and show unto you that eternal life, which was from the Father, and was manifested unto us. That which we have seen and heard declare we unto you that ye also may have fellowship with us: and truly our fellowship is with the Father, and with His Son Jesus Christ. And these things write we unto you that your joy may be full. (1 John: 1-4).

The destruction of Jerusalem in 70 A.D. is in many respects a devastating blow from which the early church has great difficulty in overcoming. Nahum Agivad views the utter destruction of the city in this way. In his description of the famous archaeological discovery known as "the burnt house." He explains more in great detail:

> Soot reigned over all, clinging to everything. It covered the plastered walls, and even the faces of our workmen turned black. There was no doubt that the fire had rampaged here, apparently fed by some highly inflammable material contained in the rooms. It may well have been some oil, which could account for the abundance of soot. The traces were so vivid that one could about feel the heat and the smell of the fire. So at least some of our visitors mentioned. It was now quite clear that the building was razed by the Romans in AD 70, during the destruction of Jerusalem. For the first time in the history of excavations in the city, vivid and dear archaeological evidence of the burning of the city had come to light. We refrained from publicizing this fact immediately, in order to keep from being disturbed in our world by visitors. Something amazing occurred in the hearts of all who witnessed the progress of excavation here. The burning of the Temple and the destruction of Jerusalem-fateful events in the history of the Jewish People-suddenly took on a new and horrible significance.[75]

The excavation of Jerusalem and the findings surrounding its destruction in 70 A.D. are not the first time unusual discoveries have been made in archaeology. Hans-Wolf Rachl recalls the unusual catch made by an Italian fisherman in 1832 when a bronze statue of Apollo was retrieved. He writes, "Near the site of the find there once stood an ancient city, Populonium. The god, which today stands in the Salle des Bronces in the Louvre in Paris got caught in a fisherman's net."[76] And thus archaeology in some fashion has always shed light on ancient places. But in regards to our history of John, the verification of the destruction of Jerusalem is pivotal. Agivad notes that coins discovered in the burned house have no date later than 69 A.D.

CHAPTER 4

By every indication John leaves Jerusalem either before the destruction of Jerusalem or no later than 70. He has probably written his gospel close to that year or a few years later. But what about the letters ascribed to him? The letters do not let us know the author directly. Irenaeus assigns the first two letters to John, the author of the Gospel. Clement of Alexandria acknowledges that this same John wrote the first letter. Tertullian and Origen also acknowledge that John the Apostle wrote the first letter. The Muratorion Canon compiled in Rome between 170 and 215 A.D. quotes from the compiler Hippolytes that John is the author of his Gospel and his epistles. The commentator John R.W. Stott looks to the previous external evidence for assigning the letters to John the Apostle and contends that the internal evidence is just as strong:

> So far, then we have suggested that the similarities
> of subject matter, style and vocabulary in the Gospel
> and the first letter supply very strong evidence for
> identity of authorship, which is not materially weak-
> ened by the peculiarities of each of the differences
> of emphasis in the treatment of common themes.
> John is not teaching new truths or issuing new
> commands, it is the heretics who are the innovators.
> John's task is to recall them to what they already
> know and have.[77]

John most likely writes his letters from Ephesus after he has left his roots of Judaism. He must have experienced both the fond memories of Jewish traditions in Jerusalem and the desire to proclaim the message of the Living Word among the dispersed Christians in Asia Minor. Gone are the days when he had his own home in Jerusalem, when he lived on the proceeds either of his fishing business or the kindness of brethren in Judea. Now he is in a Hellenistic city with Jewish and Asian influences. John is now considered an old man. With these thoughts the first letter can be addressed.

The introductory verses of this letter echo the thoughts of his Gospel. The emphasis now is more on the humanity of Christ according to the commentator Lenski. He observes that there are four statements about Jesus. Two of these statements imply a continuous effect: what has been seen and what has been heard is remembered by John. Two other statements were simply statements of fact. John says that we saw the Lord and we felt his flesh. He exposes the imaginations and delusions of the unbelievers.[78] John, as Paul does in Philippians, writes about the eternal descent or *kenosis* of Jesus from the realms of heaven to a flesh and blood existence on earth.

The citizens of Asia Minor believe in gods descending, as they demonstrate in Acts, identifying Paul and Barnabas as Hermes and Zeus. They also consider Augustus divine and worthy of a temple. John wastes no time in attacking the Christian perversion of idolatry when, as Stott phrases it, "This stress on the material manifestation of Christ to human ears, eyes and hands was of course directed primarily against the heretics who were troubling the church."[79] John is demonstrating the True God manifest in flesh and blood.

John proceeds to develop his thoughts on lines that benefit the believers in the Word becoming flesh. Belief in Christ results in fellowship and joy. John is referring to the prayer of Jesus in John 17 that the believers be one. But is a complete fellowship in this life possible? The answer is no. Therefore, John is thinking beyond the relative happiness of earthly fellowship to a divine rapture of love that only heaven brings. Stott again observes that "consummated fellowship will bring completed joy, and the eternal proclamation and historical manifestation of the Word will bring fellowship with one another, which is based on fellowship with the Father and Son and which issues in fullness of joy."[80]

After his opening remarks, John writes one of the key words of the letter: "light." The Greek word is "phos" from which English derived many words such as "photography." As Kenneth Wuest writes in his commentary, "The rule of Greek grammar is that the absence of the definite article shows quality, nature or essence and that God as a Person has a character or nature that partakes of light."[81] John uses words such as "light" in the letters in a similar way to how he uses metaphors in the gospel. Light becomes key in the battle against the Gnostic belief called antinomianism. This belief simply states that manner of life makes no difference to God. John counters this thinking when he writes, "If we say that we are having fellowship with Him and are walking in the darkness, we are lying and are not doing the truth; but if we are walking in the light as He is in the light we do have fellowship with one another, and the blood of Jesus, His Son, cleanses us from all sin" (1:6-7). John defines light in reference to moral action. There are those in Ephesus who are influenced by Cerinthus, a leading Gnostic heretic. This situation recalls the problems that Paul faced in the Colossian church regarding Gnosticism.

The summary of this ethical heresy is that Christians have no real moral obligations as the body and the spirit can act independently. One can dwell in the darkness of a sinful life and still have fellowship with God. John repudiates this cheap grace with the statement that one can indeed be excluded from the sacred fellowship, the *koinonia* of believers, and is deemed a liar by God. As Lenski comments, "John does not speak of a communion of those who walk in darkness, who lie and do not tell the truth."[82] John further states that all Christians must admit that their lives are not perfect for only then can the blood of Christ continuously cleanse their sins. The tense of the Greek verb implies that the cleansing is an ongoing action and occurs every minute of the Christian's life.

The real test of love can be found in the second chapter of this letter. John knows that the false intellectualism of the Gnostic belief excludes love for the brethren. John states that he who "hates his brother is in the darkness" (2:9). Another test of love is found in the attitude toward possessions. Gnosticism in many cases advocates a love of pleasure and draws sharp distinctions between the material and the spiritual. John is not advising the abandonment of material possessions, but tells all to remember the greater influence of the spiritual life. Certain possessions can be wrong, whether that be trust in intellectual power or the trust of material gain (2:15-17). True love (*agape*) avoids personal disdain for others and false hope in material matters. Although John had been successful in the trade of a fisherman, he never makes that his supreme goal in life. He is not advocating ascetic behavior nor is he advocating materialism. He is testing the Christian in regard to his true love, the love of Christ and the love of the brethren.

John next turns to another Gnostic heresy. The Gnostics deny the divinity of Christ, and thus they are antichrists. The last hour in I John 2:18 refers to the last epoch of time. Ross in his commentary reminds us, "It is important to remember that according to the N.T., with the coming of Christ, with His Death and Resurrection and Ascension, the last period of the world's history has begun. God has spoken His final message in His son."[83] John can see that heretics like Cerinthus only validate the signs of things to come. Those who were, are, and would be Christians experience the evil enticements of the antichrist philosophy. These Gnostic beliefs have never left the world, and to John, Christians are all his little children who can and will be tempted by false teachers. Wuest observes that these children "must not allow themselves to become entangled in the Gnostic heresy regarding the Person of the Word Jesus."[84]

In the last part of the second chapter, John advises his listeners how to avoid such heresy. He admonishes them to cling to the message that they have heard from the very beginning (2:24). As Stott remarks about those who are obsessed with the latest ideas, they "show themselves to be Athenian not the Christian." John further emphasizes the great assistance of the Spirit who would indwell us. This is the Spirit who will serve as our personal advocate or "paraclete," who will plead our case to God and interprets our innermost expressions of need (Romans 8). Stott presents the balance that the Christian must have in relying on the Holy Spirit as found in the scriptures.[85] We must remember that the Holy Spirit in John's teachings, as well as all writers of the New

CHAPTER 4

Testament, does not contradict the teachings of the gospel message in the scriptures. The Spirit helps each Christian when he prays to Christ for protection. The Spirit interprets our petitions, and He serves as our advocate and protector. When teachings such as the ones fostered by the Gnostics come, the child of God will be protected.

In chapter three of his first letter, John considers the Christian's present and future existence. John, as other New Testament writers, sees only two types of existence for the Christian, the flesh and blood of this world, and the exalted state of the next world. Unlike Eastern religions, there are no endless repetitions of earthly life, and unlike Gnostic beliefs, there are not any ladders of approach to heaven. John uses the word "know" often to emphasize his certainty of future existence. He knows that great expectations are before us: "we know that when Christ appears, we shall be like Him, for we shall see Him as He is" (3:2).

Ross defines John's attitude as "we shall be like Him, as He is now in His glory."[86] Greek society before Socrates believed in the divinity of the soul but had great difficulty with the concept of a glorified body. In John's letter he believes that Christians will become as the glorified Lord (3:2). John is a last eyewitness to the resurrected Jesus. On the shores of Galilee, John has a glimpse of what we will become. Jesus has overcome death and ascends to heaven. Wuest believes that John is talking about this physical likeness in the third chapter of the letter. Wuest is reminded of Paul's teaching in the third chapter of Philippians where the Christian's body will be changed from one of humiliation to one of glory. "We shall be like our Lord as to His physical, glorified body."[87] Stott contributes to the eternal discussion by leaning toward Paul's belief that, after death, the Christian will be in heaven with Christ. "It is enough for us to know that on the last day and through eternity we shall be both with Christ and like Christ, for the fuller revelation of what we are going to be we are content to wait."[88]

John does not explore this period between death and the *parousia* or second coming. Paul refers to going to be with the Lord. Jesus gives us the parable of the beggar in Abraham's bosom. In this letter John is more interested with the transformation in this world that constitutes the beginning of an eternal relationship with God. He also addresses the nature of one's life in preparation for the next. John warns his readers that Christians cannot remain in a lifestyle of sin (3:6). In this matter he has to confront the Gnostic heresy directly. As Ross so aptly words it, "Sin is not in the believer the ruling principle, as it is in the case of the deficient persistent sinner."[89]

To emphasize the new life, the Christian not living a sinful existence, John provides a litmus test. Does the Christian love his or her fellow Christian? "For this is the message which you heard from the beginning that we should love one another; not as Cain was of the evil one, and slew his brother. And wherefore slew he him? Because his works were evil and his brother's righteous" (John 3:11-12). Ross portrays the murder in this way, "The diabolical nature of Cain's crime came out in this, that it was his brother's righteousness and his acceptance with God that excited his murderous hate."[90]

The rest of the third chapter describes the healing and transforming power of love to the Christian who chooses not to live the life of sin. Again, John uses the word "know." He "knows" that we have passed from death to life (3:14). The Gnostic position is that knowledge alone solves life's problems, but this knowledge is available only to a select few. John is saying that true knowledge (*gnosis*) is demonstrated by true love (*agape*). John gives us the supreme example of love similar to Paul's illustration in Philippians, the second chapter. John concludes that, if Jesus gave His life for us, we should be willing to give our lives for the brethren (3:16). This is a most dramatic example to be sure, and John then offers a more common example of the brethren in need. Lenski comments, "We are children of God when we show the evidence of love in deed and in truth."[91] This chapter thus ends the quest for a sinless life by admonishing the readers to love. Individual sins

CHAPTER 4

are recognized by John, and John rejects the Gnostic claim that one cannot sin or that a lifetime of sin is acceptable. He further rejects the Gnostic belief that one can selectively love people. The child of God does not choose only the fellow intellectual as worthy of love or the person of wealth as worthy of grace. Love, according to John, is inclusive not exclusive, and is exhibited by deed as well as by word (3:18).

In chapter four John again emphasizes what true belief is. Again the Gnostic heresy must be understood. The Gnostics do not believe in the sufficiency of Jesus as Lord, nor did they believe in His humanity. Paul in the Colossian letter has to stress the completeness (*pleroma*) of Christ. Paul and John exalt Jesus as Lord rather than the Gnostics attitude of Jesus as simply one of the steps on the ladder to heaven. As a test of belief in Jesus as the Christ, John pens his ode to love in 1 John 4:7-21. John states that true love (*agape*) is shown by deed not just in thought. John places the crux of his argument with the origin of love. He writes, "Not that we loved God but that he loved us, and sent his Son to be the propitiation for our sins" (I John 4:10). The emphasis is on God as the one initiating the deed, and the Christian as the receptor. God has always been the one who does the searching for the lost souls who hide from Him.

Other verses in this chapter are essential to John's argument, including the thirteenth, where he writes that "He has given us of his Spirit." The tone of this verse is assurance coupled with the evidence of God's love. Stott adds, "By this we know that we live in him."[92] True belief produces love, and such pure knowledge, purged of the arrogance of contempt for others, assures us of God's love and of the Spirit living within us. Verse seventeen of this chapter teaches us that we have been assured to the point of boldness in the Day of Judgment. This day is described by Ross in many ways including "the last day; the day; and that day."[93] John gives us assurance for that day. Lenski concludes, "If you still fear punishment from God, you have prevented his love for you from remitting your sins and thus from planting sure confidence in your heart."[94] Or as Stott comments, we must continue our love of the individual for "it is easier to love and serve a visible human being, and thus we obtain the assurance for that day through this love, and all the while fulfilling this most basic command of our Lord."[95]

Chapter five of this letter summarizes the thoughts of John. In dealing with a heresy such as Gnosticism, John describes the struggles and faith of the Christian and compares these tenets with the weakness of this heresy. John reaffirms that the Christian must love the brethren. This love is not practiced by Gnostics who often ridicule the spiritual inferiority of their brethren. John reinforces the concept that the Christian keeps the commands of God. The Gnostics believe that behavior does not matter, and that the Christian can act in any way. John insists that conduct does matter and is basic to a proper belief in God. Wuest writes that the Christian must recognize that he is in a struggle with the forces of evil. The Christian is surrounded by these forces and must depend on God to win this incessant battle.[96]

Finally, the Christian must absolutely demonstrate faith in Jesus as the Son of God. "Who is he who is constantly coming off victorious over the world but the one who believes that Jesus is the Son of God" (1 John 5:5). This kind of faith is unknown to Cerinthus and other Gnostics. The lack of faith in the divinity of Jesus has been present in every age even among certain Christian beliefs. Wuest comments, "The combination Jesus Christ used together by John to designate one individual, is a refutation of the Cerinthian Gnostic heresy to the effect that Jesus was the person, only human, not deity, and that the Christ or divine element came upon Him at His baptism and left Him before His death on the Cross."[97]

This fifth chapter of John's first letter has always been a chapter of great confidence. John is emphatic that we know that we have eternal life. Lenski comments that John assures in order to combat the heresies of the Gnostics who denounce the way of the Christ. "The readers must know this with a clear mental perception in order to meet and to refute these Gnostic heretics when they come with the claim that they are the ones who know."[98] John also tells his readers that Jesus will hear our pleas if we ask Him according to His will (1 John 5:14).

In the closing verses of this chapter, John mentions a sin unto death. If we remember his earlier statements about sin, we are reminded of committing an individual sin in contrast to continuing in a constant state of sin. John is not counting individual sins as sins unto death, but rather a life dedicated to sin. He states that Christians do not adopt a life of continuing in sin (1 John 5:18). We have recognized that the Son of God has come and has given us true understanding that culminates in eternal life (John 5:20). As Ross observes, it is the consuming thought of John's life at this point. This is the expression that he must write once more "before he lays down his pen."[99] Stott adds, "It undermines the whole structure of the heretics' theology. It concerned the Son of God, through whom alone we can be rescued from the evil one and delivered from the world."[100]

With these closing thoughts, John presents a warning. The warning at first seems unusual. Yet the warning is certain in the context of the entire letter. Throughout this letter, John has elevated Jesus Christ as the Son of God, the one who came in the flesh to love us and to promise us eternal life. Our conduct must reflect the love of Christ in our attitudes toward others. Hatred, contempt, and discord must be banished from the Christian's life. If we continue in love, the assurance of an eternity with God will await us.

John's Second Letter

The writer identifies himself as the elder in this brief letter and to his reader as an elect lady (1:1). Commentators such as Wuest believe the lady to be a homeowner in the area of Ephesus where "her home was the meeting place of the local assembly."[101] *The*

Expositor's Greek Testament observes that it is not uncommon for a wealthy member of the assembly (such as Philemon to whom Paul wrote) to host the assembly in his own home.[102] Whether John is referring to an actual person or simply referring to the congregation as the elect lady is certainly not the most important issue of the letter. This letter again contrasts truth and love with heresy and falsehood. This particular congregation must have been experiencing the heresies of the Ephesian region. John identifies love as the mark of the Christian church: "I ask that we love one another. And this is love: that we walk in obedience to his commands. As you have heard from the beginning, his command is that you walk in love" (1:5-6). Lenski comments, "This is the spiritual love which in First John is made one of the outstanding marks of all true Christians. The antichristian heretics and deceivers have no love for the members of the true church, they try to tear it to pieces."[103]

The text of the letter expresses John's great joy that some of his children are walking in the truth (1:4). There is adequate inference in this statement that John realizes that there are some who are not walking in the truth. The love that John again talks about in this letter is in synchronization with God's commandments. John is still dealing with heresies from the first letter. Now an entire congregation has to make a decision. This congregation is besieged by those who deny Christ (1:7). As Wuest puts it, "The person, therefore, who goes beyond the teaching of the incarnation of the Son in human flesh, thus denying the incarnation, does not possess God in a saving relationship."[104]

In many ways the second letter is also a precursor to the third letter attributed to John. John is identifying those who resist the truth such as the leader Diotrophes. Lenski muses, "How all this applies to Diotrophes and to his clique is plain. He hated John himself although John was an apostle; he closed the door of hospitality to John's missionaries, threatened the members who would receive them, and opened the door to Gnostic proselytes." Later Lenski surmises, "John does not name Diotrophes in this letter to the congregation. John is not settling with the opposition by means of this letter; he is coming in person to do that."[105]

John in the second letter stresses pure doctrine in Christ over the heresies of the proud unbelievers, those who have denied Jesus Christ as Lord. John cannot tolerate this unbelief, the very essence of anti-Christian behavior (1:7-10). He makes it clear that he will uphold doctrine as well as *agape* love. The two do not exclude one another.

John's Third Letter

The third letter attributed to John is well crafted with plots and subplots. The letter is a microcosm of the first century church with parallels through the years even to the present. The letter identifies three members of a congregation: Gaius, Diotrophes, and Demetrius.

The first mentioned is Gaius, clearly a favorite of John. Gaius is a popular name in the Roman world, even used by the Caesars. This Gaius has sometimes been spoken of as the Gaius of Derbe (Acts 20:4). Although this cannot be completely verified, John commends this Gaius for his spiritual health and hopes that his physical health will improve and prosper as has his spiritual health (1:1-8). Stott observes that the prosperity gospel message, so popular through the years, is quickly disproved as this man has experienced physical difficulties while exceling in spiritual wealth.[106] Ross further comments that many are concerned about the health of their bodies, "but they never give a thought to their souls."[107]

Gaius is an extraordinary everyday Christian. He represents everyman as a Christian. John considers him to be one of the faithful spiritual children and uses the term "beloved" to express his appreciation of Gaius's life (1:2). Roberts suggested that Gaius is a convert of John. "A preacher delights to know that those whom he has converted and has helped to mature in Christ are being faithful to what has been taught." The chief contribution of Gaius is the physical and spiritual support he renders to his brethren. "Gaius was being loyal to the responsibilities of Christian love and to the truth which he had espoused, perhaps also to the reputation which he had earned among the brethren."[108]

A more striking contrast could not be shown than the daunting figure of Diotrophes found in the ninth verse. Gaius has pure, loving, and altruistic motives while Diotrophes reflects the arrogant and domineering attitudes of the Gnostics. John describes him as one who has to have his way (1:9-10). Ross thinks Diotrophes has "utter contempt of the teachings of Jesus."[109] John's mission clearly is to confront this rebellious, pompous, villain when he visits the area. Diotrophes is the leading heretic of the area and likely is one of the Gnostics who despises the truth and the true believers such as Gaius. A power struggle is taking place, and John is willing to enter the fray, knowing that truth guided by love will win.

The letter concludes with the commendation of Demetrius, a little known Christian of this congregation (1:12). Demetrius is probably better known to John as one of the faithful preachers and as a preacher who would receive the assistance of Gaius. Roberts conjectures that "the natural inference is that he was one of the traveling preachers of the gospel whom the elder had mentioned to Gaius and encouraged him to entertain. Quite likely he was the bearer of this letter to Gaius."[110]

Who will win the battle for truth in this congregation? There is no doubt. John and the forces of truth will triumph over the forces of an arrogant heresy. Lenski is right when he states that John would settle the Gnostic problem in this church personally, for John is never afraid to defend the truth. "As the apostle Paul, he was not ashamed of the gospel for it is the power of salvation not only to the Jew but to the Gentile as well."[111]

CHAPTER 4

In Conclusion to John's Letters

In summary, conservative scholars have overwhelmingly attributed the authorship of these three letters to John. David Smith in *The Expositor's Greek Testament* especially notes the similarities between the Gospel of John and his first letter. "It is beyond reasonable doubt that the Epistle and the Gospel are from the same pen. They agree in style, language, and thought." The second and third letters usually focus on John's self-description as the elder ("presbuteros") and to its meaning.[112] Smith again writes, "There is no doubt that the Second and Third Epistles are from the same hand." And in reference to the use of the word "elder" in the salutation, he adds, "The second generation of Christians used it of their predecessors, the men of early days."[113] John is one of the last survivors of the early days and confidently describes himself as the elder one.

The letters of John address all of these levels of society and his teachings have applied to each level. The letters can be summarized in these conclusive findings of truth:

1. The greatest doctrine for John is the divine and human nature of Jesus Christ. Throughout his letters John sees Jesus as the divine revelation of God. Jesus is from the eternal, yet seen with human eyes and touched with human hands. He states that Jesus is the light and without sin in contrast to the sinful nature of mankind who live in darkness. Jesus has obliterated the power from sin by the shedding of his blood, and this blood continuously cleanses the believer of the power of sin.

2. John teaches that this world will end, but those who walk in the light of Jesus Christ will live forever. Jesus has promised eternal life, although the glory of our eternal bodies has not yet been revealed. This process of eternal life has begun even while the Christian is living in this world.

3. John teaches us *agape* love. This love is divine in nature, coming from God. Agape love is love for the brethren, and indeed for all of humanity. This love is inclusive, not exclusive, and proves itself in action and not in word. This love increases the boldness of the Christian in all things righteous, and this love alleviates a sense of doubt or fear in regard to salvation.

4. The greatest sin is the denial of Jesus Christ as the Son of God. This anti-Christian spirit envelopes some of the so-called believers in these letters. This sin is secured by a false arrogant knowledge that elevates self and denies the power of Christ. The one who denies Christ also denies spiritual life to himself.

John's Life in the Later Years

As this book has had such a strong focus on the history of John, the Apostle, it would be good to review his personal journey so far. The biography has of necessity included his writings, for these writings also reflect his character. John began his ministry for Christ as a young fisherman. He was educated well for a middle class son of a tradesman. He is capable of writing and speaking his own language of Aramaic as well as Greek, the language of commerce and diplomacy. In this respect he is above average, as most of his countrymen are not able to read or write. His family is bourgeois in almost every sense and is probably part of a fishing consortium that includes Simon Peter's family. With his brother James and his mother and father very closely involved, we have the picture of a provincial and yet progressive family. In all likelihood, John in later years receives some investment income from the family business that he probably sold after the deaths of his brother and father. From all indications, he has no history of marriage, although one can never be certain in these matters for the scriptures reveal Peter's marriage only through his mother-in-law's illness in Matthew 8:14 and the comments of the

Apostle Paul. The patristic writings traditionally regard him as a celibate throughout life, and the scriptures never mention that he is married. From every indication, the apostles who remain unmarried do so by choice and not by command. Constant danger and uncertainty of the future often dictate that the single life is the better one for the apostles.

We have noticed that John is in the inner three circle of Jesus, though at first he is third on the list. Peter also assumes leadership, and James always precedes his brother in the synoptic gospel narratives. However, John becomes a strong leader and important writer for the Cause of Christ, including his contribution to the Gospels.

- Stephen Smalley, in his book *John Evangelist and Interpreter*, writes that "John did not rewrite the Synoptics but was rather preserving in his own way a Christian tradition parallel to theirs."[114] Smalley conjectures the time of writing as 80 A.D. for the early date, after John moves to Ephesus, and certainly by 70 A.D.

- The Gospel of John is different in many respects from the other three, but as Smalley indicates, "it was grounded in historical tradition when it departs from the Synoptics, as well as when it overlaps with them."[115]

- It is is a summation, a personal memoir, and an ode of love to his Christ. R.H. Lightfoot in his commentary states that it is in perfect balance with Jesus as God and man. Lightfoot remarks that it is unique in that it begins in heaven and closes on earth.[116]

John by this time has certainly been honored as one of the last links to Jesus. Certainly he would have had encouragement from the churches in the area of Ephesus to write such a gospel. At this time John assumes the role of the elder one, the honored one, a title of great respect. He becomes a fatherly figure who visits the churches surrounding Ephesus. These places in Asia Minor are well known to John. As Paul did years before, John visits cities of the region and knows the individual congregations and loves each one dearly.

Somewhere in the years 80-90 A.D. John becomes part of a larger assignment. Wayne Meeks comments that individual households in various cities recognize "being part of a larger movement." Meeks adds, "No group can persist for any appreciable time without some patterns of leadership, some differentiation of roles among its members, some means of managing conflict, some ways of articulating shared values and norms, and some sanctions to assure acceptable levels of conformity to those norms."[117]

In this situation, John becomes the paternal mentor. He, as Paul with the Corinthians and Galatians, confronts the internal and external problems of each congregation. John's robust energy belies his advanced age, and he becomes the de facto guardian of the churches of Asia Minor. He never retires from service to Christ, and he willingly assumes this mantle of leadership in Ephesus. He continues to amaze with his writings, his love for the brethren, and his zeal in dealing with the enemies of the brotherhood. As an old man, John thrives in a great metropolis, never retreating to a pleasant place of seclusion. Surely his work for the Lord is coming to an end. Yet there is more.

The Visions

> And I saw a new heaven and a new earth: for the
> first heaven and the first earth were passed away;
> and there was no more sea. And I John saw the
> holy city, New Jerusalem, coming down from God
> out of heaven, prepared as a bride adorned for her
> husband. And I heard a great voice out of heaven
> saying, Behold the tabernacle of God is with men,
> and He will dwell with them, and they shall be His
> people, and God Himself shall be with them, and

be their God. And God shall wipe away all tears
from their eyes; and there shall be no more death,
neither sorrow, nor crying, neither shall there be any
more pain: for the former things are passed away.
(Revelation 21:1-4)

When John through the Holy Spirit wrote these words, his secure
world at Ephesus had radically changed. In the year 81 A.D.
Domitian became emperor. Historian Michael Grant describes
Domitian's reign as "a meticulously thought-out policy of destruction."[118] John prospers and suffers during this emperor's rule,
which ends with Domitian's assassination in 96. Grant observes
that Domitian's last three years are full of paranoia. In Grant's ex-
tensive study of the Roman emperors, he writes about Domitian's
intensified policy to track down Jews. Furthermore, he collects an
odious tax called the "fiscus Judaicus" and condemns any people
who adopt Jewish customs, describing such practices as atheism
since these observances avoided any sacrifice to the emperor. In
his book, *The World of Rome*, Grant recognizes the change that
Christianity made, especially in the lower classes. He credits John
with incorporating Greek philosophical terms in the gospel message, and the message with offering hope, which Epicureanism
denies. This hope alleviates suffering that the "Stoics grimly
accepted."[119]

The divinity of the emperor is an idea that germinated from the
days of Augustus.[120] John is aware of this divine claim even when
living in Judea. Yet, as the apostle Paul had done, John attempts
to live under the authorities as much as possible. He has to deal
with the vacillations of the individual emperors. Augustus and
Tiberius, for the most part, cause no major problems to Jews or
Christians, but Nero finds the Christians an easy target, especially in Rome. Aquila and Priscilla feel the temporary wrath of
Claudius. Still, Paul does not lash out against Rome, which offers
him a sense of protection. John also does not seem to have any
clash with the Romans during his time of writing.

When we come to the last book attributed to John—Revelation or the Apocalypse—the enemy is clearly Rome. Christians are being assaulted with an intense persecution by the government. After years of dealing with internal problems of the church at Ephesus and surrounding cities, John is confronted in A.D. 95 with life-threatening situations. At the time of the writing of Revelation, John is in exile on the small Greek island in the Mediterranean called Patmos. Robert Wilken observes in his book, *The Christians As the Romans Saw Them*, that Domitian had "exiled distinguished citizens, accused some of his own provincial governors of conspiracy, and driven from public life good and able men. In this atmosphere of fear and suspicion good men were unwilling to speak their minds to friends lest they be implicated as traitors and summarily whisked off to exile or death."[121]

The Revelation itself has been attributed by most conservative scholars to John the Apostle. Lenski writes, "Until the time of Origen and including him the whole church knew of only one John i.e., the apostle." Lenski observes that the book contains the special wording of apocalyptic writing. "The Lord intended the language of Revelation to be different from that of John's other writings."[122] Leon Morris agrees that this John is the author saying, "Only one John was great enough among the Christians to need no description."[123] The question has always been present as to why John is chosen to be the writer. The other gospel writers could not have predicted such a choice. These writers at times focus on John's poor attitudes and the attitudes of his family. They do mention him as a member of the circle whom Christ takes into His confidence, but they do not describe John in visionary or compassionate terms. As has already been discussed, Luke in Acts 15 acknowledges that John has grown to be one of the pillars of the church. The time of this fifteenth chapter was about 50 A.D. Yet, most of John's spiritual progress is documented in his own writings.

At the age of at least 90, John seems an unlikely writer for the most mystical book in the New Testament. But all of John's life prepares him. As a Jew, he is familiar with the apocalyptic writings of the Old Testament. He has no doubt studied the writings of Daniel and Ezekiel. John is open to the mysteries of God as no other New Testament writer except Paul. And God has a plan for John even beyond the plans for the Apostle Paul. John is to receive the visions of what is to come for Christians.

These visions, aptly called the Apocalypse or Revelation, have been the subject of endless comments, speculations, and volumes. A conservative scholar, William Hendriksen has written one of the best commentaries on Revelation, *More Than Conquerors*. Hendriksen expresses the strong conviction that John the Apostle is the author, guided directly by the Holy Spirit. Hendriksen cites the traditions of the church of the first two centuries including such notables as Justin Martyr; Irenaeus; Clement of Alexandria; Tertullian; and Origen, all of whom ascribe the book to John the Apostle. Hendriksen also believes the date of authorship as 95-96 A.D. as opposed to earlier dates. "When we add to all this that according to a very strong tradition the apostle John was banished to the isle of Patmos, and that he spent the closing years of his life at Ephesus, to which the first of the seven epistles of the Apocalypse was addressed, the conclusion that the last book of the Bible was written by the disciple whom Jesus loved is inescapable."[124]

J. W. Roberts also agrees that this book is written by John the Apostle in his later years. He describes the conditions of the church at Ephesus and surrounding cities as much different from the time of Paul in the decades of the 50s and 60s. The conditions are different from the times when Peter wrote to the Christians who had just settled in Asia Minor. There are new opponents, new compromises, and new hazards including severe persecutions. There are references to indifference in some churches and to great wealth in others. Roberts also selects a later date, in the 90s, since Laodicea had materially recovered from an earthquake that Tacitus, the renowned Roman historian, records there in 60 A.D. Roberts espouses the view that John is especially concerned with the churches in his venue. Persecutions are eminent, and warnings must be issued. The emperor Domitian is to be feared.

"As the decades passed, the dark cloud on the horizon was the rise and spread of the cult of emperor worship."[125]

With these observations in mind, the first three chapters of Revelation are essential in identifying the author. Since the work is one filled with visions and symbols, what John saw at the beginning of his work that he transmitted to his readers is most important. He speaks of himself in the first chapter as the servant of Jesus Christ and the brother to the seven churches that are in Asia Minor. At this time no other writer is eligible for this claim. Peter and Paul have been martyred, according to every tradition. Only John has labored extensively with the seven churches, and only John made his residence in Ephesus for over twenty years.

John sets the tone of the letter in the first chapter when he declares his own sharing of tribulation with the seven churches. This number seven is the number of completion and perfection in Jewish writings. It becomes the first prominent symbol of the book with many more to follow. What John sees in visionary form and is told to write became the most brilliant apocalypse in scripture. He is directed to write, and the words he writes are words of prophesy. God as the Alpha and Omega gives John the authority to write. Only the Apostle John of Ephesus, who knows the seven churches intimately, could be entrusted with giving these congregations the good and bad news. Concurring with William Ramsay and other scholars, Roberts describes the prophecies as reflecting an intimate knowledge of these fellowships including the "history, topography, economics, and religious life of the cities where the churches were located."[126]

The problems of these seven churches vary. John addresses the individual needs of each one. He writes words of praise, encouragement, warning, and condemnation. The church at Laodicea has historically borne the brunt of criticism from ministers because of its wealth and inertia. Ironically, this is the city that races to rebuild itself after that terrible earthquake of 60 A.D. But there are commendable churches such as Philadelphia and Smyrna. Most congregations are in the average range such as

CHAPTER 4

Ephesus where its priorities are not as focused on Christ as in earlier times. The letters to the churches warn of impending dangers. Gone are the days of Roman protection that saved evangelists such as Paul at Corinth. In his book, *Ancient Corinth*, Nicos Papahatzis reminds us that the success of Paul's ventures in that Greek city are largely because of the magistrate Gallio's decision "that Paul's teachings did not constitute an offense under Roman Law."[127] Rather, John has to prepare his people for persecution, even death, at the hands of authorities.

The fear of death and the afterlife is of great concern to the classical world. Kenneth Dover in his book, *The Greeks*, reviews the predominant philosophies of the time. The Stoics find the soul to be some part of a greater universe, and for the Epicureans "removal of the fear of divine punishment was crucial."[128] For most of the ancient world, death is a great mystery, and future existence uncertain. Historian Robert Garland writes about the predominant view of death in the Greek mind as one where "the dead as perceived by the living were in a very literal sense mere shadows of their former selves."[129] John prepares his readers for the uncertainty of life after death. How much of John's visions are intended for the people of his day, the so-called "preterist view," and how much is intended for future generations, deemed the "futurist view," has never been solved, and will always be discussed. There can be no doubt that symbols such as Babylon refer to the dangers of Rome. The numerology of seven, twenty-four, and 144,000 was familiar to those Christians of that day who had some background in apocalyptic literature.

John sees glimpses of heaven that only Paul and Stephen have viewed. Unlike them, he gives us a much more detailed panorama of the future life. He promises his readers a final victory and a return of their Lord in triumph. John's heavenly visions include the martyrs and their white robes. He sees a new world with people from every nation, every race, and too numerous to count. He sees a city, the New Jerusalem adorned as a bride for her husband. The ancient cities are much like the cities of the modern world, full of greed and danger. The Roman writer Juvenal satirizes his city of Rome, "But here in Rome we must toe the line of fashion, living beyond our means, and often on borrowed credit."[130]

Juvenal writes of buildings collapsing, constant noise at night, and endless traffic and chaos. But John sees an idealized city where tears are wiped away and the old dangers of earthly life pass away. The symbols of this city are described as gorgeous: streets of gold, jeweled buildings, everlasting day with none of the fears of the night. The book *Heaven: A History* describes both Paul's and John's concepts of the heavenly city. For Paul another house has been prepared that houses the soul's heavenly body. This move from earth to heaven necessitates the death of the old body. For John, as well as Jesus and Paul, this heaven is God-centered. In Revelation, no natural elements such as the sun and moon are needed because of the bright light of God's eternal presence. *Heaven: A History* pictures the New Jerusalem as "designed for the blessed; imitating a temple, it served as the final place for their full and total communion with God."[131]

What is the final message of this most intriguing of apocalyptic writings? Hendriksen believes it to be ultimate victory for the Christian. "Not the Devil but Christ is victorious. God's plan though for a while seemingly-never really-defeated, in the end is seen to triumph completely. Conquerors are we. Nay, more than conquerors, for not only are we delivered from the greatest curse, yea, from every curse, but we obtain the most glorious blessing besides, Rev.21:3."[132] This message gives hope to the persecuted churches of John's time and gives hope to all Christians in future times battling the forces of evil.

After the writing of Revelation and the death of Domitian, John returns to Ephesus. Myths abound about his seeming immortality, including the story that he continues to live even while entombed. John might have had close friendships with many younger Christians such as Polycarp, who would have seen John and known his teachings.[133] He never becomes reclusive. He is the beloved disciple, the blessed believer, the spiritual father.

CHAPTER 4

His final message is one of love toward God and toward the entire world. Yet, John is always that fiery defender of Jesus Christ and the truth of Jesus' teachings. John has been underestimated for years and neglected for centuries. He lived a long life full of wonder and mystery. John is privileged to see what no other mortal had seen, and ultimately, he has blessed all generations by his life and writings.

CHAPTER 5

John the Baptist

John Prepares the Way

The relationship of John the Baptist to Jesus is one of similarities and contrasts in the scriptures. Elizabeth, the mother of the Baptist, is described in the scriptures as a kinswoman to Mary. She may be an aunt or a cousin, but not a sister. Jesus and John are, in all likelihood, cousins. John's mission in regards to Jesus is clear from the beginning. Luke 1:67-79 records a song of praise from Zechariah, John's father. The commentator Leon Morris states that Zechariah's song of praise surprises us by not beginning with John but with the Messiah who is about to come to earth. This song of praise reveals the role of John as the Baptizer who will be the prophet of the Most High, an honor not given for many centuries. John the Baptist is a forerunner to prepare the way for the Messiah. This John calls all people to repentance and tells them about the Messiah.[134]

Throughout Zechariah's encounter with the angel Gabriel, the word "joy" is emphasized. The Bible says the priest will be proud of his son the prophet. His son will be filled with the Holy Spirit. John will be filled with special powers from his birth, and he will be great, yet in subjection to a Greater One. John will change the thoughts of his countrymen, and the patriarchs will be pleased (Luke 1:11-17). Leon Morris comments, "The fathers may mean the patriarchs, the great ancestors of the present sinners. From their vantage point in the next world they looked at their descendants and were displeased. But John would bring about a change that the fathers would come to look with favor on Israel. The result would be a people prepared for the Lord."[135] Thus the angel Gabriel brought joy to the priest and his wife Elizabeth. He gives "good news" that will come with the birth of the Messiah. As previously mentioned, when Mary visits her relative after Gabriel's announcement, Elizabeth is already six months pregnant. The visit probably begins as a planned trip from Nazareth to a place in the hill country of Judea. Their meeting reinforces Mary's belief that her child will be greater than Elizabeth's child. Elizabeth greets Mary with overwhelming excitement, for she feels her own baby leap inside her. Luke adds that the Holy Spirit helps Elizabeth interpret the meaning of Mary's baby. Thus Mary, who comes to praise Elizabeth, is herself the object of praise (Luke 1:39-35). As previously noted, Morris writes, "A further point of interest is that John the Baptist did not recognize Jesus as Messiah until the baptism of Jesus. Apparently Elizabeth's recognition that the Lord was inspired was personal. John had to find out for himself."[136]

The New Testament introduces us to the Baptist as an adult in Matthew chapter three. In the same way as Jesus, a large portion of John's early years is left out of the scriptures. Matthew describes John as a man of the wilderness. His story begins "in media res," and he is pictured as a prophet of God. The commentator Alfred Plummer notes that "we do not at all know how long John was in the wilderness before he came forward as a Prophet and as the herald of the Messiah. And it is not easy to make out exactly when and where he and the Messiah came in contact with one another, or when the Ministry of the Messiah begins."[137]

As a prophet, John succeeds Malachi who had appeared some four hundred years previously, as explained further by Plummer:

> This oppressive silence had at last been broken, and once more God had a message for the nation, spoken by the living voice of a herald sent by Him and not merely recorded in the prophetic scrolls. But the message of this new Prophet was not altogether acceptable. It was a great joy that a prophet had appeared. It was indeed good tidings that the Kingdom of God was at hand. But it was not such welcome news that not every child of Abraham would have the right to enter into the Kingdom; that many of them had no better right than Gentiles had to enter into it; and that even those who were not children of Abraham could win the right to enter. What is needed to secure entrance into the Kingdom is repentance, a change of heart (*metanoia*), a fundamental revolution in moral purpose; and, as a sign and seal of this fundamental change, he required all who came to him confessing their sins to submit to the rite of baptism. It might almost be said that John had excommunicated the whole nation, and would re-admit none to communion, unless they professed, not merely sorrow for their sins, but resolution to break off from them and start afresh. As a token of this solemn change of life, he plunged them under the water, to bury the polluted past, and then made them rise again to newness of life.[138]

The Baptist is a commanding presence to those who see and hear him. J.W. McGarvey in his work on Matthew and Mark mentions that John "among all the great preachers known to history chose a wilderness as his place of preaching. All others, not excepting Jesus and his apostles, went into the cities and villages where the people could be found: John alone began and ended in the wilderness, the people going out to him instead of his going to the people."[139] His manner of life is plain, and his clothing roughhewn. He would be categorized today as an ascetic because of his camel-hair clothing and diet of locust and honey (Matthew 3:4). However, McGarvey comments that this manner of life only reinforces his austerity and perhaps adds to his charismatic appeal to the multitudes.[140]

Jesus' Baptism

When John the Baptist meets Jesus for His baptism, it is the only time recorded in the scriptures when they see each other. Plummer in his commentary remarks that popular accounts depict them as youthful playmates. However, Matthew records the rite of baptism as their only meeting. As Plummer says, John "consciously took Elijah as his model. There is the same rough garb and ascetic life, the same isolation from society and fearlessness towards it, the same readiness to rebuke either king or multitudes. The lives of both Prophets are a protest against the corruption of contemporary society. But far less than Elijah is John a despairing pessimist: his message is full of hope."[141]

This message of hope is seen in the baptism of Jesus. John knows that Jesus does not need to be baptized by him. He recognizes the superior mission of his relative (Matthew 3:14). As the narrative continues, John's value decreases and the life of Jesus takes on a superior meaning. It is one of the most humble acknowledgements of the superiority of Jesus in the New Testament. John is to proclaim the Lamb of God to the world. No longer will Jewish heritage be the defining mark of a follower of God. And thus, John continues his preaching in the wilderness.

The paths of the kinsmen do not cross again although they both minister to their followers. John attacks the social corruption of his day. Plummer reminds that John challenges the moral corruption of Herod Antipas and Herodias as Elijah had challenged King Ahab and Queen Jezebel.[142] The challenges are high, and both prophets are fearless. John's great story is told by the gospel writers in various ways. Mark's account is perhaps the most detailed and reflects upon the events that would ultimately lead to the execution of John. McGarvey notes the opinion that Mark's account of these events is "more creditable to Herod than Matthew's stating more fully the views and motives by which he was activated."[143]

The Death of John the Baptist

In clear and precise writing Mark relates the particular occasion that lead to John's demise. John, like Elijah, is not afraid to challenge the authority of a corrupt government. Jesus waits until the close of His ministry to challenge the power of Rome. John faces the power of Rome also and then is thrown in prison:

> For Herod himself had sent forth and laid hold upon John, and bound him in prison for Herodias' sake, his brother Philip's wife for he had married her. For John had said unto Herod, 'It is not lawful for thee to have thy brother's wife.' Therefore Herodias had a quarrel against him, and would have killed him; but she could not: for Herod feared John, knowing that he was a just man and a holy, and observed him; and when he heard him, he did many things, and heard him gladly. (Mark 6:17-20)

McGarvey comments that Herod's fear of the multitude "must be referred to the later period of the imprisonment, when the importance of Herodias had begun to prevail with him; and they introduce an additional restraining influence which affected him all the time, the fear of the multitude."[144]

Mark's interpretation of this story places the influence on Herodias' deep-seated hatred towards John. The intermarriage of the Herod family is a subject of continuous fascination. In most cases revenge and murder become a part of the story. One can recall that the patriarch, Herod the Great, murders two of his sons and one of his wives. Herod Antipas carries on this tradition of terror. However, John is so remarkable in his proclamation that Herod can only listen with respect. Herod considers John a prophet and a holy man.

McGarvey suggests that Herodias must have harangued Herod for some period of time. The stage is set for one of the most famous banquets in the New Testament. A birthday celebration recorded in scripture is rare indeed. Celebrations in that day lasted for days and could involve invitations to the most powerful people of the kingdom. Herodias uses the opportunity to put in place her plan of revenge. As McGarvey states, "She found the day convenient as its events transpired, and had sufficient quickness of wit to take advantage of the opportunities which it afforded."[145]

This celebration would include very powerful people. Romans as well as Jews would be there. Mark uses detailed descriptions of those present. There are "his nobles and commanders, and the chief men of Galilee" (Mark 6:21). The time is ripe for Herodias to execute her plan. She persuades her daughter to dance before the celebration party. This dance has been painted many times and is a favorite subject for the artists of the Renaissance. It is clear that the dance greatly influences Herod. He is so overjoyed that he offers the girl whatever she desires, even half of his kingdom. This young girl has to ask her mother, Herodias, what to do. The answer is succinct and horrid. "And she said, 'The head of John the Baptist'" (Mark 6:24).

The king cannot bow out. He has made a clear statement before his highest officials. His oath is final, and the executioner beheads John while he is in prison. Matthew 14:12 tells us of John's loyal disciples, indicating that John has a following. The scriptures do not specify that his followers are of a certain type, as the Zealots or the Essenes. However, they are most dedicated to their prophet and see that he is properly buried. The severed head of John is brought to Herodias. It can be assumed that the celebration ends here.[146]

John's disciples tell Jesus of John's death (Matthew 14:12), a natural notification as He is a relative. What would be His reaction? He does not demonstrate revenge but great sadness. Matthew records that He departs by a ship into a solitary place (14:13). McGarvey concludes, "Jesus himself could not fail to be deeply moved by the mournful fate of John. The cruelty of the deed, the love which he bore to the victim, the thought of his own fate which it brought to mind, and the excitement of the people, all combined to stir within him a variety of emotions."(147)

John had languished in a prison before his execution. Matthew records that Herodias had been the person who desired this. "For Herod had laid hold on John, and bound him, and put him in prison for Herodias' sake, his brother (Philip's) wife" (Matthew 14:3). Before his execution, John goes through a period of depression, similar to the mood of Elijah. John not only questions his role as a prophet, but the role of Jesus.

While in prison, John sends disciples to Jesus. These disciples echo the words of John, "Art thou He that comes or do we look for another?" (Matthew 11:3). Jesus answers John with the words of His mission statement in Nazareth, "The blind receive their sight, and the lame walk, the lepers are cleansed, and the deaf hear, the dead are raised up, and the poor have the gospel preached to them" (Matthew 11:6, 7). McGarvey states his opinion of John's thinking in this way: "Looking, as John did, in common with all the Jews, for an earthly king in the coming Messiah, and seeing in Jesus no aspiration for such a position, he was so far confused as to think that while Jesus fulfilled a part of the promise, there might be another Coming One who would fulfill the remainder."(148)

In answering John's question, Jesus verifies His mission as spiritual rather than earthly. He also confirms the great opportunity that has been given John and says, "Among them that are born of women there hath not risen a greater than John the Baptist" (Matthew 11:11). Jesus also acknowledges the limitations of John's mission. John will not enjoy the Kingdom. He will be viewed

CHAPTER 5

differently as a prophet who did not live among the people. He will be considered by some as having a devil. Jesus eats and drinks among the people, and He too is criticized as possessed of a devil. They share much in this life.

As the story of John the Baptist ends, his influence is great and his disciples are even teaching his beliefs in the Book of Acts. John is considered charismatic by many and possessed by others. His style of living is unlike other personalities, including Jesus. He is reclusive, confrontational, and fearless. He initiates the change that is completed by Jesus. Perhaps he is the least under-stood of Jesus' earthly family.

CHAPTER 6

DESCENDANTS

Descendants of Mary

Other immediate relatives of Jesus are not prominently mentioned in the New Testament, including other brothers and sisters. The question of descendants has arisen over time. This question is determined by the interpretation of the family composition. Most scholars agree that Joseph and Mary, as a married couple, have children after the miraculous birth of Jesus, using the aforementioned Matthew 1:25 as reference. This would include His brothers, the most prominent being James and Jude. His family also includes other brothers and sisters. Thus the likelihood of descendants from the mother of Jesus is possible. If one takes the view that Mary has no other children than Jesus, then the maternal line ends.

If Mary has other children, her descendants might survive for generations. The earthly part of Jesus' DNA could survive even into modern times. Again, if one believes the scriptural doctrine of the "only begotten" son of God, then the DNA of Joseph, the legal father, does not play any part in future descendants.

Jesus' Respectful Relationships with Women

A more intriguing question has appeared recently and merits some discussion. In the New Testament Jesus is always portrayed as an unmarried male throughout His earthly life. Yet, some have questioned the Biblical account. They would postulate that Jesus must have married. However, The New Testament renders these arguments as specious. Jesus reaches out to women in a very spiritual way. He appeals to the righteous and the unrighteous, the rich and poor, women and men. The relation of Jesus towards other women is always that of a Rabbi, a Messiah, a teacher, and a healer. The important point to remember is that Jesus treats women with an equal respect as He does men.

In the eighth chapter of Luke, several women become His followers, and they contribute to His ministry. This loyalty would be unusual in that time. Rubel Shelly in his book, *A Jewish Savior Through Gentile Eyes*, comments, "Women were often regarded as property in antiquity. A woman was a father's to barter; he would get the best price he could for himself in arranging her marriage. Rabbis did not include women as their disciples. Some regarded it as a sin to teach women."[149] Shelly gives several examples from Luke as evidence of the respect that Jesus has for women. He forgives sins of prostitutes, He resurrects a female child, and He heals a woman who had spent her money on physicians with no results. But perhaps His greatest contribution, according to Shelly, is that He teaches women, includes them as His disciples, and points out certain women as examples of sacrificial living.[150] The women who contribute to His ministry are a varied lot including a government official's wife and a woman healed of evil spirits. These women include Joanna, Susanna, and Mary Magdalene, and they are to be disciples of Jesus and part of the traveling band that accompanies Him on occasion.

Shelly notes "women were witnesses of his resurrection."[(151)] One of these women disciples is Mary Magdalene who is the first witness of the resurrected Christ. Mary of Magdala is one of these devoted women who becomes a disciple. Magdala can easily be seen from the Sea of Galilee today. Louis Sweet in an article in the *International Standard Bible Encyclopedia* suggests that her character has been maligned as an evil person instead of a victim of demon possession. "Had this always been understood and kept in mind, the unfortunate identification of Mary with the career of public prostitution would have been much less easy. She was a healed invalid, not a social derelict."[(152)]

Mary is the first to recognize the resurrected Jesus. She is overcome with emotion. After all, Jesus is the one who healed her of demon possession. Her tender scene of recognition includes the word "Rabboni" or Rabbi. The apostle John records a warning given by Jesus to Mary not to clasp Him (20:16-17). Godet interprets the warning of Jesus as such: "but Jesus declares to them by this message of Mary that He is not yet ascended, and that it is only now that He is going to ascend."[(153)] Godet interprets the word "them" as the other disciples. Thus the picture is one of Mary overjoyed and wishing to grasp the feet of her Rabbi. Jesus, however, says that He must first ascend to His father before this can happen. The complete picture of Mary is one of a devoted disciple to the unique Rabbi and Savior. He is more than a mortal man to her for He exhibits all the powers of the Messiah. As Sweet describes her, she "is characteristic of woman at her best."[(154)]

The other women who spend significant time with Jesus reside in the village of Bethany. Sweet recalls the passage in Luke 10 where the reader is introduced to the family of Martha and Mary. The sisters are of different personalities. Martha is a leader, absorbed with organization and who, according to Sweet, finds "adequate and satisfying expression at all times in the ordinary kindly offices of hospitality and domestic service."[(155)] Mary, on the other hand, is "inward, silent, brooding, with a latent capacity for stress and the forewith, unconventional expression of feelings, slowly gathering intensity through days of thought and repression."(156)

The closing scenes that the New Testament scriptures provide of these remarkable women are found in the Gospel of John. John remembers the resurrection miracle that Jesus performed at the home of Mary and Martha. After their brother Lazarus dies, Martha says to Jesus, "If you had been here, my brother would not have died. Yet even now I know that God will do anything you ask." Jesus told her, 'Your brother will live again.' Martha answered, 'I know that he will be raised to life on the last day, when all the dead are raised'" (John 11:21-24).

Then Martha makes one of the most profound statements in the New Testament. "I believe that you are Christ, the Son of God. You are the one we hoped would come into the world" (John 11:27). Martha then alerts her sister Mary. "'The teacher is here, and He wants to see you.' As soon as Mary heard this, she got up and went out to Jesus. Mary went to where Jesus was. Then as soon as she saw him, she knelt at his feet and said, 'Lord if you had been here, my brother would not have died.' When Jesus saw that Mary and the people with her were crying, He was terribly upset and asked, 'Where have you put his body?' They replied, 'Lord come and you will see.' Jesus started crying, and the people said, 'See how much he loved Lazarus'" (John 11:28, 32-26).

Of course Jesus resurrects Lazarus, and the story ends with much happiness, as previously noted. What can be overlooked is the profound respect that these sisters have for Jesus. Martha calls Him "the Christ, the Son of God." She also refers to Him as "the teacher." Mary expresses her respect for Jesus by kneeling at His feet. Later in the John 12:1-11, Mary takes a bottle of expensive perfume and pours it on the feet of Jesus. She then wipes His feet with her hair, an overwhelming show of respect.

When these prominent women of Jesus' ministry are observed, their attitude is that He is no ordinary person; He is the unique Rabbi or the Messiah. The gospel writers do not express any feelings beyond this reverential attitude toward Jesus. Romantic fallacies from non-scriptural sources are simply fallacies.

Jesus sees His role as the Son of God who would leave *spiritual* descendants. The Apostle John writes, "My dear friends, we are already God's children, though what we will be hasn't yet been seen" (I John 3:2). Jesus says, "I won't leave you like orphans, I will come back to you. In a little while the people of this world won't be able to see me, but you will see me and because I live, you will live. Then you will know that I am one with the Father" (John 14:18-20).

CHAPTER 6

CHAPTER 7

In Conclusion

The family of Jesus consists of very different personalities such as Mary, His mother, and Joseph, His earthly father. His brothers James and Jude are devout Jews who later acknowledge Jesus as the Messiah. They become important figures in the early years of the church and both write significant letters of the New Testament canon. In addition, James is responsible for harmony in the Christian fellowship.

John the Baptist, a kinsman, is a bold preacher and prophet who prepares the people for the mission of Jesus Christ. He is the first martyr mentioned in the New Testament. James and John, also kinsmen of Jesus, are evangelists. James is an early church martyr. John, his brother, is an early missionary and a companion evangelist with Peter. He then becomes a leader of the Jerusalem church. In later life he moves to Ephesus and, according to tradition, lives to an advanced age. There he writes his gospel and letters. After exile to Patmos Island, he writes the apocalyptic Book of Revelation.

Jesus leaves as His descendants all who believe and obey Him. His descendants are many in number and are believers from all periods of time and from all races and ethnicities. For as the Messiah and Savior of humanity, He brings all men and women to His heavenly Father.

CHAPTER 7

NOTES

1. Louis Sweet, "The Genealogy of Jesus Christ," *International Standard Bible Encyclopedia*, Wm. B. Eerdmans Publishing Company, Grand Rapids, Michigan, 1960

2. Ibid

3. Ibid

4. A.B. Bruce, "The Synoptic Gospels," *The Expositor's Greek Testament*, Wm. B. Eerdmans Publishing Company, Grand Rapids Michigan, 1956

5. Ibid

6. Louis Sweet, "The Genealogy of Jesus Christ," *International Standard Bible Encyclopedia*, Wm. B. Eerdmans Publishing Company, Grand Rapids, Michigan, 1960

7. Ibid

8. Ibid

9. Leon Morris, "Luke," *Tyndale New Testament Commentaries*, Inter-Varsity Press, Wm. B. Eerdmans Publishing Company, Grand Rapids, Michigan, 1999

10. Ibid

11. Ibid

12. Ibid

13. B.F. Westcott, *The Gospel According to St. John*, Wm. B. Eerdmans Publishing Company, Grand Rapids, Michigan, 1958

14. Ibid

15. Leon Sweet, "Mary," *International Standard Bible Encyclopedia*, Wm. B. Eerdmans Publishing Company, Grand Rapids Michigan, 1960

16. F.F. Bruce, *The Acts of the Apostles*, The Tyndale Press, London, 1956

17. Leon Morris, "Luke," *Tyndale New Testament Commentaries*, Inter-Varsity Press, Wm. B. Eerdmans Publishing Company, Grand Rapids, Michigan, 1999

18. R.T. France, *The Gospel of Matthew*, Wm. B. Eerdmans Publishing Company, Grand Rapids, Michigan, 2007

19. Leon Morris, "Luke," *Tyndale New Testament Commentaries*, Inter-Varsity Press, Wm. B. Eerdmans Publishing Company, Grand Rapids Michigan, 1999

20. J. W. McGarvey, *The New Testament Commentary*, Vol.1 Matthew and Mark, Gospel Light Publishing Company, Delight, Arkansas, 1875

21. Leon Morris, "Luke," *Tyndale New Testament Commentaries*, Inter-Varsity Press, Wm. B. Eerdmans Publishing Company, Grand Rapids Michigan, 1999

22. Alfred Plummer, *The Exegetical Commentary on the Gospel According to S. Matthew*, Wm. B. Eerdmans Publishing Company, Grand Rapids, Michigan, 1956

23. John Painter, *Just James: the Brother of Jesus in History and Tradition*, University of South Carolina Press, Columbia, South Carolina, 1997

24. F.F. Bruce, *The Acts of the Apostles*, The Tyndale Press, London, 1956

25. Scott McKnight, *The Brother of Jesus: James the Just and His Mission*, John Knox Press, Louisville, 2001

26. F.F. Bruce, *The Spreading Flame*, The Paternoster Press, London, 1961

27. J.W. Roberts, *The Letter of James*, The Sweet Publishing Company, Austin, Texas, 1977

28. Ibid

29. Ibid

30. John Painter, *Just James: The Brother of Jesus in History and Tradition*, University of South Carolina Press, Columbia, South Carolina, 1997

31. J.R.W. Stott, *The Message of Acts*, Inter-Varsity Press, Downers Grove, Illinois, 1990

32. R.B.Rackham, *The Acts of the Apostles*, Metheun and Company, London, 1957

NOTES

33. F.F. Bruce, *The Spreading Flame*, The Paternoster Press, London, 1961

34. Ibid

35. R.B. Rackham, *The Acts of the Apostles*, Metheun and Company, London, 1957

36. Eusebius, *Ecclesiastical History*, Hendrikson Publishing, Peabody, Massachusetts, 1998

37. J. B. Mayor, "The General Epistle of Jude," *The Expositor's Greek Testament*, Wm. B. Eerdmans Publishing Company, Grand Rapids, Michigan, 1956

38. W.E. Oesterley, "The General Epistle of John," *The Expositor's Greek Testament*, Wm. B. Eerdmans Publishing Company, Grand Rapids, Michigan, 1956

39. F.F. Bruce *New Testament History*, Doubleday, Garden City, New York, 1980

40. Ibid

41. Eusebius, *The Ecclesiastical History*, Baker Book House, Grand Rapids, Michigan, 1991

42. Wayne A. Meeks, *The First Urban Christians*, Yale University Press, New Haven, 2003

43. J.W. Roberts, *The Letter of James*, The Sweet Publishing Company, Austin, Texas, 1977

44. Frank Pack, *The Gospel According to John*, The Sweet Publishing Company, Austin, Texas, 1977

45. Ibid

46. B.F. Westcott, *The Gospel According to St. John*, Wm. B. Eerdmans Publishing Company, Grand Rapids, Michigan, 1958

47. Frederick Godet, *Commentary on the Gospel of John*, Zondervan Publishing Company, Grand Rapids, Michigan, 1886

48. Salvatore Nappo, *Pompeii: A Guide to the Ancient City*, Barnes and Noble, New York, 1998

49. Wayne A. Meeks, *The First Urban Christians*, Yale University Press, New Haven, 2003

50. Jerome Murphy-O'Connor, *The Holy Land*, Oxford University Press, Oxford, 1986

51. Steven Runciman, *The History of the Crusades*, Cambridge University Press, Cambridge, 1968

52. Frank Pack, *The Gospel According to John*, The Sweet Publishing Company, Austin, Texas, 1977

53. Ibid

54. Marcus Dods, *The Expositor's Greek Testament*, Wm. B. Eerdmans Publishing Company, Grand Rapids, Michigan, 1956

55. Frank Pack, *The Gospel According to John*, The Sweet Publishing Company, Austin, Texas, 1977

56. Ibid

57. B.F. Westcott, *The Gospel According to St. John*, Wm. B. Eerdmans Publishing Company, Grand Rapids, Michigan, 1958

58. Ibid

59. Frank Pack, *The Gospel According to John*, The Sweet Publishing Company, Austin, Texas, 1977

60. B.F. Westcott, *The Gospel According to St. John*, Wm. B. Eerdmans Publishing Company, Grand Rapids, Michigan, 1958

61. Steven Runciman, *The History of the Crusades*, Cambridge University Press, Cambridge, 1968

62. Frank Pack, *The Gospel According to John*, The Sweet Publishing Company, Austin, Texas, 1977

63. B.F. Westcott, *The Gospel According to St. John*, Wm. B. Eerdmans Publishing Company, Grand Rapids, Michigan, 1958

64. James Orr, "Jesus Christ" The *International Standard Bible Encyclopedia*, Wm. B. Eerdmans Publishing Company, Grand Rapids, Michigan, 1960

NOTES

65. B.F. Westcott, *The Gospel According to St. John*, Wm. B. Eerdmans Publishing Company, Grand Rapids, Michigan, 1958

66. Frank Pack, *The Gospel According to John*, The Sweet Publishing Company, Austin, Texas, 1977

67. Frederick Godet, *Commentary on the Gospel of John*, Zondervan Publishing Company, Grand Rapids, Michigan, 1886

68. Frank Pack, *The Gospel According to John*, The Sweet Publishing Company, Austin, Texas, 1977

69. B.F. Westcott, *The Gospel According to St. John*, Wm. B. Eerdmans Publishing Company, Grand Rapids, Michigan, 1958

70. Ralph Gower, *The New Manners and Customs of Bible Times*, Moody Press, Chicago, 1987

71. Marcus Dods, *The Expositor's Greek Testament*, Wm. B. Eerdmans Publishing Company, Grand Rapids, Michigan, 1956

72. Ibid

73. B.F. Westcott, *The Gospel According to St. John*, Wm. B. Eerdmans Publishing Company, Grand Rapids, Michigan, 1958

74. Ibid

75. Nahman Avided, *Discovering Jerusalem*, Thomas Nelson Publishers, Nashville, 1983

76. Hans Wolf-Rackl, *Discovering the Past Archaeology under Water*, Charles Scribner, New York, 1968

77. J.R.W. Stott, *The Letters of John*, Wm. B. Eerdmans Publishing Company, Grand Rapids, Michigan, 1996

78. R.C.H. Lenski, *The Interpretation of I and II Epistles of Peter, The Three Epistles of John, and The Epistle of Jude*, Augsburg Publishing House, Minneapolis, 1969

79. J.R.W. Stott, *The Letters of John*, Wm. B. Eerdmans Publishing Company, Grand Rapids, Michigan, 1996

80. Ibid

81. Kenneth Wuest, *In These Last Days*, Wm. B. Eerdmans Publishing Company, Grand Rapids, Michigan, 1957

82. R.C.H. Lenski, *The Interpretation of I and II Epistles of Peter, The Three Epistles of John, and the Epistle of Jude*, Augsburg Publishing Company, Minneapolis, 1969

83. Alexander Ross, *The Epistles of James and John*, Wm. B. Eerdmans Publishing Company, Grand Rapids, Michigan, 1974

84. Kenneth S. Wuest, *In These Last Days*, Wm. B. Eerdmans Publishing Company, Grand Rapids, Michigan, 1857

85. J.R.W. Stott, *The Letters of John*, Wm. B. Eerdmans Publishing Company, Grand Rapids, Michigan, 1996

86. Alexander Ross, *The Epistles of James and John*, Wm. B. Eerdmans Publishing Company, Grand Rapids, Michigan, 1974

87. Kenneth S. Wuest, *In These Last Days*, Wm. B. Eerdmans Publishing Company, Grand Rapids, Michigan, 1957

88. J.R.W. Stott, *The Letters of John*, Wm. B. Eerdmans Publishing Company, Grand Rapids, Michigan, 1996

89. Alexander Ross, *The Epistles of James and John*, Wm. B. Eerdmans Publishing Company, Grand Rapids, Michigan, 1974

90. Ibid

91. R.C.H. Lenski, *The Interpretation of I and II Epistles of Peter, The Three Epistles of John and The Epistle of Jude*, Augsburg Publishing Company, Minneapolis, 1969

92. J.R.W. Stott, *The Letters of John*, Wm. B. Eerdmans Publishing Company, Grand Rapids, Michigan, 1996

93. Alexander Ross, *The Epistles of James and John*, Wm. B. Eerdmans Publishing Company, Grand Rapids, Michigan, 1974

NOTES

94. R.C.H. Lenski, *The Interpretation of I and II Epistles of Peter, The Three Epistles of John and the Epistle of Jude*, Augsburg Publishing Company, Minneapolis, 1969

95. J.R.W. Stott, *The Epistles of John*, Wm. B. Eerdmans Publishing Company, Grand Rapids, Michigan, 1996

96. Kenneth Wuest, *In These Last Days*, Wm. B. Eerdmans Publishing Company, Grand Rapids, 1957

97. Ibid

98. R.C.H. Lenski, *The Interpretation of I and II Epistles of Peter, The Three Epistles of John and the Epistle of Jude*, Augsburg Publishing Company, Minneapolis, 1969

99. Alexander Ross, *The Epistles of James and John*, Wm. B. Eerdmans Publishing Company, Grand Rapids, Michigan, 1974

100. J.R.W. Stott, *The Letters of John*, Wm. B. Eerdmans Publishing Company, Grand Rapids, Michigan, 1996

101. Kenneth Wuest, *In These Last Days*, Wm. B. Eerdmans Publishing Company, Grand Rapids, Michigan, 1957

102. David Smith, *The Expositors Greek Testament*, Wm. B. Eerdmans Publishing Company, Grand Rapids, Michigan, 1956

103. R.C.H. Lenski, *The Interpretation of I and II Epistles of Peter, The Three Epistles of John, and The Epistle of Jude*, Augsburg Publishing Company, Minneapolis, 1969

104. Kenneth Wuest, *In These Last Days*, Wm. B. Eerdmans Publishing Company, Grand Rapids, Michigan, 1957

105. R.C.H. Lenski, *The Interpretation of I and II Epistles of Peter, The Three Epistles of John and The Epistle of Jude*, Augsburg Publishing Company, Grand Rapids, Michigan, 1969

106. J.R.W. Stott, *The Letters of John*, Wm. B. Eerdmans Publishing Company, Grand Rapids, Michigan, 1996

107. Alexander Ross, *The Epistles of James and John*, Wm. B. Eerdmans Publishing Company, Grand Rapids, Michigan, 1974

108. J. W. Roberts, *The Letters of John*, Sweet Publishing Company, Austin Texas, 1968

109. Alexander Ross, *The Epistles of James and John*, Wm. B. Eerdmans Publishing Company, Grand Rapids, Michigan, 1996

110. J.W. Roberts, *The Letters of John*, Sweet Publishing Company, Austin, Texas, 1968

111. R.C.H. Lenski, *The Interpretation of I and II Epistles of Peter, The Three Epistles of John, and The Epistle of Jude*. Augsburg Publishing Company, Minneapolis, 1969

112. David Smith, *Expositors Greek Testament*, Wm. B. Eerdmans Publishing Company, Grand Rapids, Michigan, 1956

113. Ibid

114. Stephen S. Smalley, *John: Evangelist and Interpreter*, Intervarsity Press, Downers Grove, Illinois, 1998

115. Ibid.

116. R. H. Lightfoot, *St. John's Gospel*, Oxford University Press, Oxford, 1972

117. Wayne A. Meeks, *The First Urban Christians*, Yale University Press, New Haven, 2003

118. Michael Grant, *The World of Rome*, Mentor Books, New York, 1960

119. Ibid

120. Ibid

121. Robert Wilken, *The Christians As the Romans Saw Them*, Yale University Press, New Haven, 2003

122. R.C.H. Lenski, *The Interpretation of St. John's Revelation*, Augsburg Publishing House, Minneapolis, 1961

123. Leon Morris, *The Book of Revelation*, Wm. B. Eerdmans Publishing Company, Grand Rapids, Michigan, 1999

124. William Hendrickson, *More Than Conquerors*, Baker Book House, Grand Rapids Michigan, 1970

125. J.W. Roberts, *The Revelation of John*, Sweet Publishing Company, Sweet Publishing Company, Austin, Texas, 1974

NOTES

126. Ibid

127. Nicos Papahatzis, *Ancient Corinth*, Ekelotike Athenon, Athens, 2001

128. Kenneth Dover, *The Greeks*, The University of Texas Press, Austin, Texas, 1986

129. Robert Garland, *The Greek Way of Death*, Cornell University Press, Ithaca, New York, 1985

130. Juvenal, *Juvenal: The Sixteen Satires*, Penguin Books, London, 1974

131. Colleen McDannell and Bernhard Lang, *Heaven: A History*, Yale University Press, New Haven, 1988

132. William Hendriksen, *More Than Conquerors*, Baker Book House, Grand Rapids, Michigan, 1970

133. Frederick Godet, *Commentary on the Gospel of John*, Zondervan Publishing Company, Grand Rapids, Michigan, 1886

134. Leon Morris, "Luke," *Tyndale New Testament Commentaries*, Inter-Varsity Press, Wm. B. Eerdmans Publishing Company, 1999

135. Ibid

136. Ibid

137. Alfred Plummer, *An Exegetical Commentary on the Gospel According to S. Matthew*, Wm. B. Eerdmans Publishing Company, 1956

138. Ibid

139. J.W. McGarvey, *The New Testament Commentary, Vol. I Matthew and Mark*, Gospel Light Publishing Company, Delight, Arkansas, 1875

140. Ibid

141. Alfred Plummer, *An Exegetical Commentary on the Gospel According to S. Matthew*, Wm. B. Eerdmans Publishing Company, Grand Rapids, Michigan, 1956

142. Ibid

143. J.W. McGarvey, *The New Testament Commentary, Vol. I Matthew and Mark*, Gospel Light Publishing Company, Delight, Arkansas, 1875

144. Ibid

145. Ibid

146. Ibid

147. Ibid

148. Ibid

149. Rubel Shelly, *A Jewish Savior Through Gentile Eyes*, 20th Century Christian, Nashville, Tennessee, 1990

150. Ibid

151. Ibid

152. Louis Sweet, "Mary Magdalene," *International Standard Bible Encyclopedia*, Wm. B. Eerdmans Publishing Company, Grand Rapids, Michigan, 1960

153. Frederick Godet, *Commentary on the Gospel of John*, Zondervan Publishing Company, Grand Rapids, Michigan, 1886

154. Louis Sweet, "Mary Magdalene," *International Standard Bible Encyclopedia*, Wm. B. Eerdmans Publishing Company, Grand Rapids, Michigan, 1960

155. Louis Sweet, "Mary of Bethany," *International Standard Bible Encyclopedia*, Wm. B. Eerdmans Publishing Company, Grand Rapids, Michigan, 1960

156. Ibid

NOTES

ABOUT THE AUTHOR

James Byers is a graduate of David Lipscomb College, magna cum laude, and teaches an Asian Bible class at Harpeth Hills Church of Christ where he serves as a deacon. He has been a minister in congregations in Tennessee, Georgia, and Florida. He had a career with the State of Tennessee as a teacher in Williamson County and with the Department of Human Services. He is married to the former Marie Potter, and they have one son, Tracy Byers, who is married to the former Evie Wade. James and Marie are also proud grandparents of three grandchildren. This is his fifth book.

FINAL COMMENTS

I would like to pay tribute to the Hilliard Press staff for their work editing and designing this book.

I want to make mention that several different Biblical translations were used in the book.

Finally, many portions of this book are a compendium of my other books, which are listed in the pages following this one, specifically *John: The Blessed Apostle* and *James, the Brother of Jesus*. Some of the material from this book comes verbatim from my other works, as pieces of those texts fit perfectly within the topic of this one. If you'd like to read a more in-depth account of John and James, you can visit the Hilliard Press website or contact me directly to purchase other books.

Thank you to my readers,

James Byers

OTHER BOOKS BY THE AUTHOR

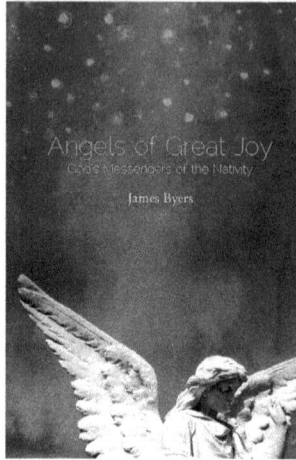

Angels of Great Joy: God's Messengers of the Nativity
ISBN 978-0-9860244-1-2

The New Testament begins with an explosion of heavenly messengers—angels of joy with glorious announcements. Angels told of the birth and parts of the infancy narrative. These proclamations came to the humble of spirit: a country priest, lowly shepherds of Bethlehem, a Galilean carpenter, and a maiden from Nazareth. Filled with hope, comfort, and praise to God, the promises shared a beautiful truth: the fulfillment of Isaiah 9:6. "Unto us a child is born...His name will be Wonderful."

To order copies, contact the author or visit
www.hilliardinstitute.com.

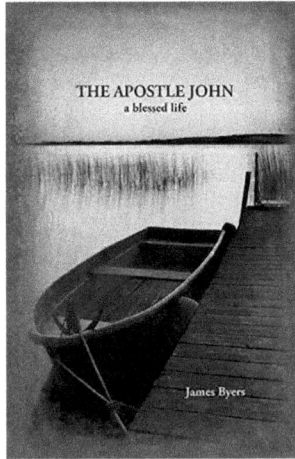

The Apostle John: A Blessed Life
ISBN-13: 978-0-9800285-2-2

The Apostle John: A Blessed Life takes a historical and philosophical look into the life and work of this son of Zebedee. Once a "son of thunder," John's spiritual journey led him to become the man called to write a special, personal account of the life of Jesus. This book guides the reader through the world in which John lived and the gospel, letters, and revelation tale written with divine direction and his unique perspective.

From his days fishing with his father and brother on the Sea of Galilee, to his travels with Jesus, and finally to his last days writing and sharing Christ's word in Ephesus, this apostle truly lived a blessed life.

To order copies, contact the author or visit
www.hilliardinstitute.com.

JAMES BYERS

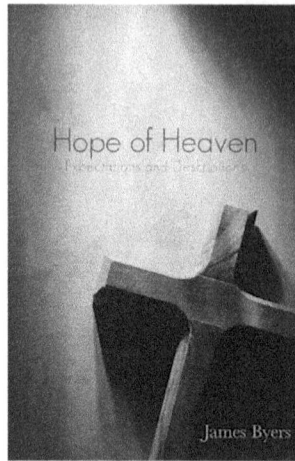

Hope of Heaven
ISBN 978-0-9822618-7-3

"I have prepared a place for you, in My Father's house where there are many dwelling places" (John 14:2). With these words Jesus encouraged His disciples, and future Christians, of a glorious heaven. His first coming made this hope of heaven possible; His final coming will make it complete. This book explores some of the expectations and descriptions of heaven throughout the Bible. Christ will come. His eternal kingdom shall be established. This is the great hope and fear of all generations.

To order copies, contact the author or visit
www.hilliardinstitute.com.

OTHER BOOKS BY THE AUTHOR

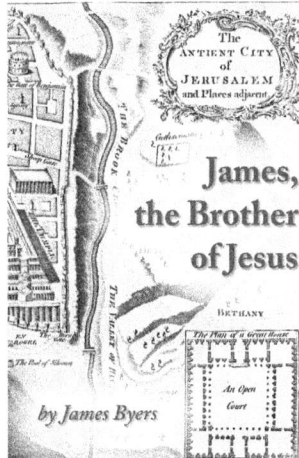

James, the Brother of Jesus
ISBN 978-0-9912792-8-9

Though *James, the Brother of Jesus*, began his life doubting the Messiahship, he ended with a strong confidence and a great social conscience towards the needy of body and soul. He became the most visible of the leaders of the Jerusalem church, a mentor and adviser to the great evangelists of his time. In 2002 an ossuary was discovered in Israel allegedly containing the remains of James the brother of Jesus. This discovery led to a renewed interest in this rather obscure person and his contributions to early Christianity, and this book covers biblical references, commentaries, and other research on this man who exercised great humility towards God and his fellow Christians accompanied with a great zeal towards the salvation of the lost souls of his generation.

"My friends, if any followers have wandered away from the truth, you should try to lead them back. If you turn sinners from the wrong way, you will save them from death" (James 5:19-20a).

To order copies, contact the author or visit
www.hilliardinstitute.com.